UYOMA HEROES AND GLADIATORS

By

LWANDE ONEKO

Copyright © 2015

All rights reserved by **Lwande Oneko**

No part of this book may be reproduced or transmitted in any form or by any means, graphic, electronic, or mechanical including photocopying, recording, taping or by any information retrieval system, without permission in writing of the publisher.

Ariba Book Publishers

P.O Box 503-40600

Siaya –Kenya

Website: www.aribabp.com

Email: admin@aribabp.com

ISBN: 978-9966-1856-6-2

First published 2015

Printed by: Susmo Enterprises

P.o Box-345-00511

Nairobi

ACKNOWLEDGEMENT

This book would not have been possible without the co-operation and assistance of so many people. It is impossible to name everybody who has contributed to the final work, but to them all I owe my gratitude.

We want to pay special gratitude to the following informats: ex-political detainee Mr.Apollo Washingtone Juma Otito, who was the forerunner in the idea of writing the Uyoma history,

Special thanks to Onyango Radier for the moral support and readiness to share his past. Special thanks to Sam Ligongo a.k.a Lord Mawira for getting his time to join us in other special research errands.

Forgetting a humble man like Jaduong' Ogaja Opanga is impossible. I thank and feel for our publishers, Ariba Book publishers Elisha Otieno, the linkman and their staff. Benjamin Ogola Luo is one man who walked us to and around the site of Owila's homestead famously known in the village as Gunda Uyoma in Alego Kobare and talked to us as if he lived with Owila, the Uyoma Patriarch.

My memmory cannot fade without mentioning the name of Uyoma son-in-law and one of the longest serving journalists in Kenya; this is none other than gigantic, heavily bi-spectacled Leo Odera who knows Uyoma like the back of his hand.

Other valuable key informants include; Mzee Mariko Odipo, Mzee Zakayo Abonyo Oyombe, Ex-chief Elisha Haggai Angira, John Ooro Oluoch, Mwalimu Alex Odie Ngure, Walter Nyawanda Ajugu, John Anyumba Nyamor, Japuonj Bob Amala, Jared Ogweno Oyugi,Mzee John Milambo, Willis Ogola Okendo, Wilson Odoyo Ochiel, Nelson Waka, Ogweny Odande, Mama Lois Christine Anyango Oneko ,Silvia Odede and Mama Doris Abonyo Owenda, Apollo Owiti Njiri of Asembo Konyango for invaluable information on the history of Jo-Uyoma and the geneology of the Dilang's in Asembo and Uyoma.

My special thanks to Dr. Nick Ogolla of Maseno University, Dr.Ongong'a Achieng' of Technical University for availing all the required literature for the production of this book. Dr. Paul Otiende Amollo was a motivator and inspiration to the development of this book.I thank him for his moral and material support.

I also acknowledge the immense moral support extended and especially to those who attended the validation workshops; James Owuor Aduda, Grace Nyawanda, Oscar Abonyo, Edwin Oyier Ogolla, Nam Oneko, Jabes Oduol Were, Agripa Ojuka Makedi, Abner Odeny, Geoffrey Atanda, Odongo Onyango, Oscar Adhiambo, Nahashon Ong'iro K'Ong'iro, Samson Odhiambo, Erick Makasembo, Henry Gero Okwiri, Pym Otieno Okwiri, Peter Oyaro Awich, Benard Owigo, Michael Odera, Elizabeth Anyango Omondi, Debborah Akinyi Odede, Harun Ouro Oyuga, Charles Otieno Ogonda, Daniel Odongo Nyandwa Chiefs; Cosmas Onyango Okwama, Charles Jomo Ajwang', Wilberforce Oyucho, Henry Ouko Otieno, Dr.Nick Ogolla and Jared Andhuong'o Alindi.

Mention need also to be made of the moral support from the Uyoma Secondary School's History and Government Teachers - Mrs.Pessila Opondo Ogeta, Oyomba George Opiyo, Gumba Evans, and Nicholas Opiyo amongst others.

I also acknowledge the following on their artistical work in promoting the book through music; composer, Jack Owenda, Promoter, musicians; Benard Ouma-Ous Jalamo, Stephen Ojee Ambeto wuod wuod Nyarawila, Lucas Ochieng Jaluthi okew gi Osare, Obong'o Sangalati wuod Ong'ielo, Owenga winyo wuod Oduol, George Oyaro Tinga, Akuga Toto, Caren Ajwang' and Doris Owenda.

I owe our deepest gratitude to the following ladies who served us delicious traditional and exotic meals during the validation workshop and documentation; Loyce Anyango Oneko, Phoebe Kola, Margret Odwar and Susan Achieng'

My deepest gratitude to Mr Hesbon Kola Midundo aka Ongwang' who tirelessly coordinated the visitations to the informats. And lastly, to Mr Henry Ouma Opiyo and Evance Otieno (wuod Akala), Pst. Shadrack George Ocholla wuod Obong'o and Ruth Owuor who helped in the documentation.

CHAPTERIZATION AND PAGINATION - (TABLE OF CONTENTS)

1. COVER PAGE
2. ACKNOWLEDGEMENT -III
3. INTRODUCTION -VI
4. THE SUMMARY- PG 1
5. GENESIS OF THE LUO- PGN 4
6. CUREENT STATUS OF THE LUO IN KENYA -– PG 7
7. THE OWILA FAMILY TREE- PG 8
8. OWILA'S OFFSPRINGS EXODUS AND SETTLEMENT PG 12 -24
9. THE GENESIS OF UYOMA -PG 23
10. THE TURBULANCES OF JO-UYOMA -PG 31
11. THE FINAL SETTLEMENT IN UYOMA- PG 43 – 50
12. THE UYOMA ASSIMILADOS- PG 49
13. THE COMING OF THE WHITE MAN- PG 54
14. TURMOILS IN UYOMA- PG 64
15. CULTURAL CHARACTERISTICS- PG 76
16. THE LEADERS, HEROES AND GLADIATORS – PG 86
17. INTERESTING STORIES FROM UYOMA – PG 114
18. SHRINES AND HISTORICAL SITES- PG 120
19. THE UYOMA ANTHEM- PG 128
20. FACILITATORS- PG 129
21. SUCCESS CORNERSTONES PG 133
22. REFERENCE BOOKS -PG 134

1. INTRODUCTION

"Okune Okune ng'isa kuma ne onyuolae?, Okune Okune nyisa kuma ne onyuolae?"

Okune Okune show me where I was born? Okune Okune show me where I was born?

"Roots, Roots, roots, where is my home, my family, my clan, my community, my nation, my race, where are my origins? Where is my ancestral land, where was my urmbilical cord buried? That is my God given right to know and to cherish.

My son Ramogi asked his grandfather as they flew mid-air with Kenya Airways from Nairobi to Kisumu and their destination was Uyoma, their ancestral land.

Ramogi *"Grandpa wapi kwa makina Yesu*?(Grandpa where is Jesus abode)"

Grand-father. "Boy it is not here"

Ramogi *"Grandpa you told me that your mother and father died and they went to heaven, where are they staying?*

He was only seven and naïve but isn't true that these questions are often asked by our children and grand children

When they came back from Uyoma I welcomed Ramogi at our Buruburu home in Nairobi, he looked at me and told me. "Daddy Buru Buru in Nairobi is not a home, It is a house; HOME is Uyoma, Uyoma Kabudha *An Ja-Kosewe, Ja-Kunya.*" I told him that he was right. 'Uyoma is home' from that day his mother nick named him Ja-Kabudha

When my father Ramogi Achien'g Oneko died, my grandson asked me "Will Babu (Great Grandfather) come back to play with me?'

I explained to him that when people die, they go to heaven but they never come back to earth. Death is but a transition from physic to spiritual land and the soul lingers on. In a second I remembered that they can come back but they can only come back when you are told their stories and those stories remain in the corridors of your mind. That is how history and stories have been handed over from generation to generation.

In my over 60+ years I have been fortunate to fully interact with five generations; my grandfather Oneko Nyauchi, my father Achieng Oneko, my peers, my son Ramogi Oneko and then my grandson Lewis Ramogi.

And so my grand father Oneko Nyauchi told me many stories about World War 1. My grandfather always talked about the World War 1 with a lot of bitterness and passion, to him it was a war he never understood. He also remembered the fierce German soldiers and their supremecy in the battlefield. He called them *Ojiro Nya Amande*. He painfully recounted the carrier corp experience where the uneducated carried luggages. The war influenced him to take his off-springs to school regardless of gender, and hence our clan's education endevour. He planted plenty of fruits and sugar cane by the lake. He enjoyed being with me, his youngest grandson who could follow him to the lake side orchard. While he was milking; grazing and doing other domestic undertakings I would stick around for many things from fruits, food and protection. He never believed in witchcraft, he encouraged modern technology while upholding Luo tradition and culture. Wealth creation was his greatest desire; he always said that people (men and women) must be financially self suffient through-out their life. My grandmother Leah Nya Nyagaya was his greatest disciple; she died a financially self suffient woman aged 92.

My father Ramogi Achieng' Oneko shared with me his MAU MAU experiences. I was part of his history having lived in three Detention Camps with him in 1959, 1960 and 1961. These were in Marsabit, Kapsabet and lastly a stink of six months in Uyoma. He lived for Kenya's Freedom from the colonial yoke and later the struggle for a Democratic Kenya. He made me live in politics all my life and before. This has influenced my political activities that I have cherished and loathed at the same score.

I have lived with my peers for more than sixty years of my life, they influenced my teenage life and later the struggle for democracy in Kenya during the Kenyatta and Moi regime. What I remember dearly are the teenage dances, the gang fights in the Nairobi estates, the University of Nairobi riots in the 1970s and a slow down of social and political activities at my marriage to bring up a family and follow my grandfather's foot steps. I moved to my grand-father's philosophy of independence and wealth creation.

My son Ramogi (named after my father) lived with me through part of the Kenyatta regime up to 1978 and the Moi regime up to the 1990s. He was with me during Coup de detat of 1982 and he died in 2001. My wife Joyce and my three daughters shaped and moulded my life to what Iam today as I write this book; I wish to thank them for their moral and material support.

My grandson "Ramogi" Lewis (named after my son Ramogi), we shared our experiences on the 2007/2008 Post Election Violence (PEV) experiences. He remembers the violent neigbouring Kibera youths who ruled the streets of Nairobi for more than two months in the dawn of 2008. When my neighbor Hon. Mugabe was shot he is the one who woke us up as he shouted said, "*grandpa, watu wa kibra wamerudi* (Grand daddy, the Kibera guys are back)". I have played and enjoyed my grandchildren's company; Ndhaye, Shema, Jojo and Zawadi

I could have sat with my children and grandchildren and told them these stories.but l also did not know the stories. Cultural heritage and stories are usually shared verbally from generation to generation. Verbal narration of these stories evaporates and change form but when they are written and documented, they can form a better basis for reference or research and further improvement and deeper understanding.

I am writing this book to narrate the story of Uyoma for the present youth and future generation. I would like them to understand and uphold their cultural heritage. I would also like them to fill the gaps that I have left and carry out research to improve and add value to Jo Uyoma History, Story, Heroes and Gladiators.

It has taken along journey to write this book. It all started when Washington Apollo Juma Otito brought me rough notes he wrote for me to start writing the book in 2005, we thought about it with my wife, but my pen was dry until yesterday in February 2014 when something ignited and motivated me to write and I started the story like this.

Just before starting, I called Hesbon Kola Midundo and Jack Owenda to join me in this boat. I am glad the boat has sailed from shore to shore of Jo Uyoma peninsula; we have driven from corner to corner, walked from home to home and then door to door. From morning to evening, from evening to night until dawn to the wee hours of the night.

And so, 'there are people who come to this world with nothing and go back with nothing.' The bible says and I quote the Bible *"Naked a man comes from his mother's womb and as he comes, so he departs. He takes nothing from his labour that he can carry in his hand."* Ecclesiastes 5:15

"But there are also some people who come to this world with nothing but they leave behind many dents which even panel beating and spraying cannot cover."These poople change the environmental terrain and infrastucture, they influence Socio-Economic trends, they carry out religious crusades, they create political turmoils and change peoples' world view; they develop and innovate scientific and technological machinery, tools and equipments.

These are the galant heroes and gladiators that Uyoma wants to celebrate and document the dents and achievements that they left behind to make Uyoma a better place to live in. That is the history and story that has been handed over from generation to generation. We have inherited this ancestral land through the great effort made by these men and women.

This is the History and story of Uyoma Heroes and Gladiators as narrated by Uyoma elders, gentlemen, ladies, boys and girls. This is a homegrown document told and written by Jo-Uyoma. I had the passion to write and I still had the passion to document this book. This passion motivated me to influence all the people who ave contributed to its final part.

Jo-Uyoma have been known for their bravery and confidence which has made them win some battles but on the same score, they have also suffered immense defeat in the name of bravery. They have been known to be defiant to authority and taking the law into their hands which has a plus and a minus. For many years until the recent past they have not held new ideas such as the coming of the Whiteman, religious organizations such Missionaries, Muslims and even clothes among others. To demonstrate this there is a saying that Ja-Uyoma could not tie a blanket. *Onget a ngeta tam Ja-Uyoma bolo.* For many years there were very few religious denominations and organizations in Uyoma until the recent past. During my childhood we would walk to St. Peter's Chianda A.C.K. church which is over ten kilometres from our home in Kunya. I followed my mother, my anties Dokya and mama Christabel odinga. I knew that Jesus came from Maseno and I had great hopes that one day he may visit Ranalo. I nicknamed him *Yesu wuod Nyar Maseno.*

Against all odds and their defiance of authority, it is a fact that in the current century Uyoma has the most modern and digital infrastructure and fast growing shopping centres compared to most parts of Kenya. Other modern development include water system, electrical infrastrature, irrigation of horticulture, all weather roads and tarmacked roads that cover every corner of this magnificent peninsula resembling an onion. From a Siaya County cereals granary it has now become a modern agricultural hub with products such as tomatoes, water melon and a variety of vegetables and fruits grown through modern irrigation technology.

Jo-Uyoma have built modern houses in their homes. These mansions are competing Nairobi high class estates such as Muthaiga, Westlands and Karen. Grass thatched houses are history into the archives and museums in the Uyoma scenary surrounded by the gentle lake Victoria known as Nam Lolwe and known as Nalubaale in Luganda. The lake was named after Queen Victoria by the explorer John Hannington Speke; he was the first European to see this Great African Lake in 1858. This was long after my Great Great grand father Osewe had settled at the present Yawo Kosewe in Chianda in Uyoma after the exodus from Kanyamwa in the mid 19th century.

THE SUMMARY

This a summary of the journey of this book

The Uyoma Heroes *Thuondi* who are listed here below are *Uyoma people known as Jo-Uyoma* who made significant contributions or great achievements that benefitted Jo-Uyoma and hence humanity. The gladiators are great warriors, skilled fighters who laid their lives in various battle fields to defend Jo-Uyoma, their wives and children, their property and the ancestral land. Most of the gladiators left behind no families of their own. Instead they left evalasting cultural heritage.

PRE- COLONIAL

From 1500 AD to 1899 AD
The movement from Got Ramogi to Thurmony (Uyoma)

Omia Ramul

The journey of Jo-Uyoma from Got Ramogi to the present Uyoma at Thurmony *Madiany* was led by Omia Ramul the son of Ramogi Ajuang'

Dilang' Wuod Odhiriany

The journey from Thurmony (Madiany) present Uyoma to Kawango was led by Dilang' **who** was the eldest son of Odhiriany

The turbulances in Kawango

Omolo Ng'ongo

When Jo-Uyoma lived among their kin in Kawango, the notorious Omolo Ong'ongo' created bad blood between Jo-Uyoma and Jo-Kawango by drowning Kawango children in to the River Wuoroya. The name originated from the Luo word *OYUMA* meaning jokes. Omolo was notorious for silly jokes and bad games including playing with his peers bad games in the river that ended up drowning them. *OYUMA* was his nickname. The Kawango people in their poor pronounciations of Luo words pronounced *OYUMA* as *UYOMA*. The Luos taunted Omolo by pronouncing his nick name the Kawango way UYOMA hence the name UYOMA.

The directive to the ancestral land, Home is best

Owila wuod Odhiriany

Owila was the leader of Jo-Uyoma during their stay in Kawango, until their exit. He died and was buried in Alego at the present Gunda Uyoma in Uyoma village-North Alego Location in 1730 AD. He directed his kins men towards Got Naya which was the ancestral Land, the burial site of Omia Ramul the son of Ramogi Ajuang'.

The return to the ancestral land from Kawango

Osike Kirina

The return of Jo-Uyoma to Thurmony was marked by many squabbles and battles with the neighbours.

Osike Kirina was instrumental in these battles and was supported by Ang'asa wuon Obor, Odero Pende Ariyo and Ramogi Okoko. They drove Jokanyidoto, JoKochia, JoKanyada, JoKakan and JoKopole out of Uyoma.

Exodus to Kanyamwa in 1790 AD

Midega Ralong'o

During the Jo-Uyoma exodus to Kanyamwa, the first group was led by Midega Ralong'o they followed the southern *Milambo* route passed Got Naya through Wikwang' through to Kanyamwa. He was assisted by Otieno Auma, Mbuge Odeny.

Life in Kanyamwa

Onyango Wuon Otonde

During the time Jo-Uyoma stayed in Kanyamwa they were faced with many battles and the leaders were Onyango wuon Otonde, Oguta Wauga, Nyawanda and Opedhi.

Preparation and return to the ancestral land

Oguta Wauga and Onyango wuon Otonde

The trip back to Uyoma entailed several rituals and the lead persons in carrying these rituals were; Onuko carried the hen with seven eggs *swi marateng kod tonge abirio,* Atieno Nyar Ahono took them to the top of Got Naya. Geke brought the striped bull *Ruath Rapenda* in his canoe.

Other notable persons in these ritual activities were:

Abiero wuod Menya (Jakajore) donated the striped bull *Ruath rapenda*

Nyawanda Haya (Jakabudha) donated the hen with seven eggs

Oguta Wauga (Jakatweng'a) donated the white (castraded) bull *Ruath Rachar Mabuoch*

Atieno Nyar Pambo the wife of Opedhi whose placenta *Bieche* was used to re-capture Uyoma

The time to recapture the ancestral homes *between 1868 - 1870 AD*

Yongo Awang' Mach and Osike Kirina

The return to Uyoma involved battle with Jo-Asembo and Jo-Sakwa. The gladiators were led by Yongo Awang' Mach and Osike Kirina the magician (Jabilo). They were assisted by their Leaders and warriors. The notable ones were Oguta Wauga, Onyango wuon Otonde, Oginga Agidhi, Andhoga the magician, Oluga Dipondo, Onoka Maugo, Nyambuoro, Omondo Adhura and Ongoro Nyapende among others.

THE COLONIAL ERA

(1890 to 1963)

Prediction of the coming of the Whitemen
Mboga Wuon Otieno

He was the Uyoma leader *Jatelo kata Ruoth* after *Ruoth* Oginga Agidhi. Before the arrival of the Colonialists *Ombogo Jarachar/Joingereza*, he had rapport and linkages with external leaders such as the Kabaka and Mumia and even the Arabs; he predicted the coming of the Whitemen

THE MUMBO MASSACRE

The British Military onslaught from 26/27 December 1899 AD.

OLuoch Abaki and Molo Nyadundo

The military on-slaught by the British on the Uyoma people is known as the Mumbo massacre at OLuoch Abaki's home. This caused the death of many innocent people, leaders and gladiators. The gladiators that are memorable are Molo Nyadundo, Obara Kadawo, Otieno Osogo, Malago Pacho, Ogundo Liech, Ragwar, Oluga Dipondo, Malago Kombe, Ogutu Anyieche, Monye Okuku and Agunga Wuon Oyola. Among the leaders that died was OLuoch Abaki.

THE DAWN OF INDEPENDENCE

(1963 to 1974)

Jonathan Okwiri

The dawn and agitation for independence was led by Jonathan Okwiri at local and National levels. The struggle for Independence was championed at National and International level by Ramogi Achieng' Oneko Owando Kwach, Nyakech OLuoro Chuodho and Fanuel Walter Odede Obonyo Rachilo Wuod Obonyo at Regional level there were Dickson Mbogo Okello, Dickson Oruko Makasembo, Owadgi Agutu *wang'e chiegni gi dholo,* Odundo Nyar Ouma, Onyango Radier among others.

INDEPEDENCE AND AFTER

(1974 TO 2014)

The later heroes and gladiators include Ouma Okendo, Odeny Ngure, Pamela Mboya, Elizabeth Ongoro, Onyango Radier, Chadwick Adongo, Jael Oriwa, Oneko and Prisca Auma among others

THE GENESIS OF THE LUO

I come from Kunya Ka -Osewe in Uyoma, Rarieda District and in Siaya County one of the fourty seven Counties in Kenya. The story of Uyoma comes from the origin of the Luo speaking Nilotes; this is what I wish to refer to as the Genesis of the Luo.

The history of the Luo people of Uyoma, for the purpose of this book will touch on the Genesis from Egypt among the Pharaohs who were originally black Nilotes hence the Arab word Sud meaning black. This is therefore the origin of the word Sudan from the Arabic word *Sud.*

Somewhere between 12th and 16th centuries A.D the Arabs from Egypt had started infiltrating the Sudan and started causing a lot of social and economic disruptions to the black pastoral and farming communities who lived in Nubia.

The black pastoralists who were Nilotes were left with a few choices in the advent of Arabs.One, Stay put fight the hostile Arabs and defend their territory, estates and heritages amidst eminent death and destruction. Two organize themselves into strong armed states in order to contain the disruptions; like the Shiluk and the Keira did and migrate away from the troubled scene, as the southern Luo, of present day Kenya, Uganda and Tanzania chose to do.

The Luo of Nyanza in Kenya and Mara District of North Eastern Tanzania are said to have come from Sudan through Uganda.

At the time of their departure, they lived at a place called Wau at the junction of Maridi River and Sue, but were under the Nubian Empire before.

The Egyptian pressure scattered them to the East, West and South.

The Western group moved and settled amongst the Black Sudanic communities such as Ghana, Chad, Nigeria and Senegal and across the Oceans to distant Lands.

Some Luos crossed the Red sea and travelled to India and China, possibly in company of the Indian and Chinese traders and disappeared into the Far East.

According to Ugandan historian, Alenyo George William, he says that there are many places and people named "LUO" in Asia. Such place includes River Luo, Luo Man Hotel in Chengdu and Luo Hu Hola in Shenzhen.

A great poet called Gao Zhi, wrote a famous poem to the goddess of the Luo River in China.

It is also argued that amongst the people who occupied the New World before Columbus particularly USA and Mexico, Brazil were the proto-Luo who migrated from the Nile Valley through west Africa in pursuit of security, wealth and other opportunities in the Americans.

In his book, "*In the proper season*" Amerigo Vespucci, later wrote that it is quiet feasible to cross the Atlantic Ocean near the Equator from Africa to South America in small open canoes.

The Luos were attracted to West Africa by the stories of gold, Silver, and plenty of land.

The Luos are believed to have been responsible for the building of the great terbenacles of Mexico and the Earth mounds and Temples of Lousiana.

Christopher Columbus and Olonzo Nino were surprised to find the black Africans with large ships heading to West Africa. Africans were navigating the Atlantic Ocean before Christ. Refer to the book titled; *"THE AFRICAN PRESENCE IN ANCIENT AMERICA, THEY CAME BEFORE COLUMBUS."*

Turning back to the Kenya, Uganda and Tanzanian Luos are termed as the Jii-speaking group, others being the Jiiang' (or Dinka) the Naath (or Nuer) and the Shilluk. The Dinka, Shilluk and Naath remained and still live in South Sudan.

The Kenyan Luo together with their cousins, who remained in Uganda are Jii-speaking Nilotes, they are the Acholi, Lang'o, PaLuo, Jonam and Alur, they all represent the Southern wing of the Jii-speakers. Others are found in the Eastern part of the Democratic Republic of Congo while others live in Egypt and Ethiopia.

The Kenyan Luos ar related to the other Nilotic clusters and this includes the plain Nilotes who are the Maasai, Samburu, Teso and Turkana. The second group is known as the Highland Nilotes and they are Kalenjins. Although the Kenyan Luo Nilotes are Jii-speaking groups, the other two have different dialects. The Plain Nilotes are the Maa speaking Nilotes. The highland Nilotes are the Kale speaking Nilotes; this group includes the Kipsigis, Nandi, Turgen and Marakwet among others.

The Luo people and dialects of their language have historic roots starting from the River Nile Delta on the Northern side into the Red Sea and along the Nile Southward across Egypt, into Sudan and then Eastern Africa inclusive of Congo, Ethiopia and then around the Lake Victoria Basin. Their roots are more prominent across the Lake Victoria region especially Uganda, to day this area is refered to as the Great Lake Region

Through history the Luo of Kenya have socially interacted and they were greatly influenced by the Buganda, Bunyoro, and Toro kingdoms among other communities.

In Kenya the Luo have closely interacted with four major neighbours namely the Nandis, Luhyas, Kipsigis and the Abagusi, before venturing and intermingling with other Kenyan communities in the other parts of Rift valley, Central Province, Coast, Nairobi Northern and Easten Kenya and the Great lakes region at large.

The Historians claim that the origin of the Kenyan Luos can be traced from Wau in southern Sudan. This I also know because as I have worked in Egypt, Sudan and South Sudan I could clearly see and hear the Luo tone in them, the black, or sud, but more prominently the Nilotic fever in them. Some say that some went West-wards towards Nigeria across the Oceans with out trace. Others say that others spread East-wards to Asia into China and Mongolia and disappeared into the bleak. I know Researches will follow these movements and document the history and trace their roots.

The first Luo arrival in Kenya is sometime around 1500 and they came in about five waves arriving at different times and these are the main groups:

- ✓ The Jo-Kajok(who migrated from Acholiland in Uganda spread from Bunyala,Samia to Yimbo near Got Ramogi then to Alego,Sakwa and then Uyoma and Asembo.The group comprised the Jo-Nyakach,in Usonga,Jo-Alego in East Alego,Jo-Karachuoyo,Jo-Kabondo and Jo-Karapul in Alego.

- ✓ The Chwanya cluster included; Jo-Kadem, Jo-Karungu, Jo-Kabuoch and Jo-Kanyamwa in Uyoma.

- ✓ The Jo-Kowiny migrated from Padhola and moved through Samia-Bugwe.they included the Kadimo, Jo-Kowili and Wanyenjra.They moved to Yimbo.

- ✓ The Jo-Komolo migrated from Pawir and arrived later. They are related to Jo-Koch,Jo-Koyo of Padhola and the Abafafoyo of Marachi.They include the Jo-Karapul of Alego,Jo-Boro,Jo-Puny,Jo-Kakan,Jo-Kager and the Kale and Kakia of Asembo and the Jo-Gem.

- ✓ The Abasuba, a heterogeneous group in Southern Nyanza were Bantus from Buganda and Busoga were assimilated into groups of Jo-Kaksingri,Jo-Kasgunga,Jo-Kaswanga,Jo-Gwassi and the Kamsingri amongst others,

This is the earliest Luo history by the historians, there are various versions and contradictions, but the above groups are known to many historians. The history or the story of Jo-Uyoma in this book is clear and we start from Got Ramogi and for this matter Ramogi the second Known as Ramogi Ajuang' as the Great-Great-Great Grand-Father of Jo-Uyoma or the patriach. He is known as Ramogi II.

THE CURRENT STATUS OF JO-LUO IN KENYA

Today the Kenyan Luo tribe or nation consists of 28 groups known as 'JO' which means the people to a particular group or area; some are related some are not related, while others are assimilated, they are further divided into various clans, sub-clans and then families. The list of the 28 Groups are as follows:

1. Jo-Gem
2. Jo-Yimbo
3. Jo-Ugenya
4. Jo-Seme
5. Jo-Kajulu
6. Jo-Karachuonyo
7. Jo-Nyakach
8. Jo-Mumbo (including Jo-Kasipul & Jo-Kabondo-both descendants of Rachuonyo)
9. Jo-Kisumo
10. Jo-Kano
11. Jo-Asembo
12. Jo-Alego
13. Jo-Uyoma
14. Jo-Sakwa
15. Jo-Kanyamkago
16. Jo-Kadem
17. Jo-Kwabwai (a group that is said to have originated from the Baganda family called Bwayi)
18. Jo-Suba/ Abasuba (comprises its own subclans, which are invariably called Jo-Chula i.e. people from Mfangano, Rusinga, Remba, Takawiri islands; Jo-Gwassi; Jo-Kaksingri; Jo-Muhuru etc.)
19. Jo-Suna (a group that was formerly Bantu but has assimilated fully into Luo. Some people classify them under the Luo Suba clan)
20. Jo-Kasgunga
21. Jo-Kanyamwa
22. Jo-Kanyada
23. Jo-Kanyidoto
24. Jo-Kamgundho
25. Jo-Kamagambo
26. Jo-Ramogi
27. Jo-Karungu
28. Jo-Kopole

I can trace my self from the 13th group among the 28 clans that form the Luo nation in Kenya. Now I want to trace my root among Jo-Uyoma.

THE OWILA FAMILY TREE

Do you know your family tree and origin?

Let me try mine. For me, I start with the first clan. I come from Kunya, Kunya is in Rageng'ni, and Ragen'gni is in Uyoma Kabudha, Kabudha is in Uyoma, Uyoma is in Rarieda, Rarieda is in Siaya, Siaya is in Kenya.

My clan is Ka-Osewe clan known as Jo-Kosewe from Kunya, *Kunya nind gi lepi*, (Kunya sleep when you are fully dressed). From Osewe I come from the house of Muche Nya-Ajemo. Muche is the third wife of Osewe. Muche had two sons these are Robi and Nyauchi. Robi had two sons and the sons are Nyawanga and Nyandwa. Nyauchi is my Great Father. Nyauchi had one son his name is Oneko. Oneko is my Grand father and I am the son of Achieng' Oneko. This Ramogi Achieng Oneko is the known freedom Fighter known as the Kapenguria Six, together with Jomo Kenyatta, Bildad kaggia, Paul Ngei, Kungu Karumba and Fred Kubai.

When we were young we used to be told that if you are not sure of parental origin then ask Okune okune *"Okune okune wach na ni thurwa nikanye"*. Incidentally the bird would turn its head to a direction and that was supposedly the origin or home of your paternal parents.

How about you? Do you know your roots? Or are you similar to the Internaly Displaced Persons (IDPs) in Kenya during the Post Election Violence PEV) of 2008. During this violence I was lucky to be involved in dispatching the IDPs from various parts of Kenya in Kisumu where most of the victims did not know their original homes, Some of them were simply guessing the possible homes. One of them told me that she was married in Alego near Rageng'ni. These are people who delinked themselves from their families and relatives. When you disassociate yourself from your family and clan you are lost in the wilderness. Remember your family is your first business on earth. Anybody who does not look after his offspring is ungodly it is written in Holy Books. In the Bible, **1Timothy 5:7, 8** Give the people these instructions, too, so that no one may be open to blame. If anyone does not provide for his relatives, and especially for his immediate family, he has denied the faith and is worse than... *Puonj ji chikno....obed maonge bura.Ka nga'to ok nyal rito joode ,to en ng'at ma osekwedo.... Kendo orach moloyo...*

We should also look at the books of **Numbers 26** Where God asked Moses and Eleazar son of Aaron to take the census of the Israelites.**Luke 3: 23 – 38,Mathews 1:1 - 17** tells us about the genealogy of Jesus Christ. Apostle Paul in all his apostolic letters starts with introducing himself in a geonological manner so that he may be known. In the book of **Acts** especially in chapters **22 vs 22 – 29**, Paul gives his defence in a genealogical reference.

My brother Dr. Ongong'a Achieng' told me that while he was studing in Russia he was challenged by his girlfriend to sing a Luo Folk song in DhoLuo. From that time he started thinking about his roots very seriuosly. If you do not know your roots you are equivalent to a man without a shadow or worse if you cannot speak your Mother or Father Tongue, then you are lost in the wilderness. The other day I was watching Equity Bank Foundation function and during the speeches one thing surprised and amused me. The German, the British and Japanese Ambasedors all started their speeches in Kiswahili. I am equally surprised at women and men who marry other World Communities and they cannot speak either languages. If you do not know your roots then you should findout from your parents or next of kin. It is parental responsibility to educate children on their roots, if your parents do not educate you, find out for yourself for the sake of your future generation. *Yawa puonjri dhou kata matin, kata penj Okune okune.*

JO-KOSEWE CLAN

Jo-Kosewe occupies the Kunya peninsula, my friend Omamo Kodande refers to Kunya as the Cape of Good Hope *Sori mar geno*. The main families who occupy Kunya Kosewe are Jo-Kosewe, Jo-Kanyawanga, Jo-Kogundo and other assimilados. These families have lived in harmony in Kunya since the beginning of the 19th Century. Surely Kunya is the Cape of Good Hope, because for it is my ancesteral home and the cradle of cultural heritage for me. It is from here that my grandfather Oneko was forcefully recruited into World War 1 in 1914. Then after the War he came back and settled in Kunya and the growth towards western education emerged amidst fertile land of plenty. Then came the education of my uncles, they all went to Chianda School then they graduated to the most prestigious schools like Maseno, Yala, Kamagambo among others. Christianity flourished later in Uyoma amidst opposition from Jo-Uyoma and all the other members of Uyoma. Later they came to understand and Christianity flourished and religious structures emerged. The first Church was St. Philip's initiated by Odinga Nya Nyandawa the mother of Jo-Kodande family and Jedida Okuku Nyo Owino, the mother of the Oneko family and then other religious structures sprung, The first permanent houses started emerging in 1940s with my uncle Oracha Nyawanga from Ajemo family, who was a fish monger taking lead followed by the first teacher in Kunya Dida Bonyo from the Abonyo family. The Osewe clan is where Mbogo Okelo comes from, we used to refer to him as the naked truth, this is because he led the naked demonstration in Kisumu mentioned in this book, he was the fore runner of Kenya's Independence and known as Chief Uhuru. Today as I write this book, the ten kilometers radius is flooded with electricity, it has its own water system, Hospital, primary and secondary school, Churches, agricultural irrigation, its own beach and fish landing bay. It has all weather road and adjacent to the great tarmac road infrustrature that engulf the Uyoma peninsular. This is where the urmblical code of my ancestors have been buried since 17th Century starting from Got Naya to Kunya Ko-Sewe. Three families form Jo-Kosewe and these are the three wives of Osewe, these wives are Abonyo, Ojode and Muche. In mid 19th century Osewe settled near Ranalo on the short cut to Aram at Dago with a natural water pan which was known as Kosewe, this place is known as Kit- Pala and now better known as Ager. This is where Osewe was buried and the remnants of his relatives were left here they are Joka Akelo of Kawere hence Jo Kabudha at the boundary with Katweng'a of Koyoo clan. They are living together with Kajore and form part of Ochieng'a Sub location. Although Yao Ko-Osewe was renamed, the original Osewe bears the name because of his settlement after the exodus from Kanyamwa as a young man in the mid 19th century. It is his father Ocharo the son of Onyango Otonde who was in the exodus. It is worth noting that Otonde was born in Uyoma, lived in Kanyamwa and returned to Uyoma. The following sons of Osewe were born at Ranalo and they include Nyauchi, Robi, Oyuga, Okongo' and Mbawi among others. Later Jo-Kosewe moved to Rageng'ni and Nyauchi later moved to Kunya. Oneko was born around Rageng'ni 1880. In 1914 Oneko Nyauchi was forcefully recruited into the first worldwar as Carrier Corps. He moved from Rageng'ni to Kunya after his return from World War1. He first settled near Kunya Primary School and now his offsprings and other siblings occupy the cape Kunya. The table below shows the Ko-Osewe clan.

JO-KOSEWE CLAN

	WIFE NUMBER 1		WIFE NUMBER 2		WIFE NUMBER 3		
Osewe's 3 Wives	OJODE	OJODE	ABONYO	ABONYO	MUCHE	MUCHE	MUCHE
Current Offsprings	OSEWE	OTIENO	OPERE	AGWENGE	LWANDE	ORACHA	ODHIAMBO
1	Osewe	Otieno	Oiko	Oyuga	Lwande Oneko	Gero	Odhiambo
2	Ojode	Ogonda	Okelo	Ouro	Achien'g Oneko	Oracha	Odongo
3	Osewe	Ouya	Anumo	Ouro	Oneko Nyauchi	Nyawanga	Nyandwa
4	Oyuga	Okong'o	Mbawi	Mbawi	Nyauchi Osewe	Robi	Robi
5	Osewe Ochar	Osewe Ochar	Osewe Ochar	Osewe Ochar	Osewe Ochar	Osewe Ochar	Osewe Ochar

Let us look at Jo-Kosewe relatives while referring to the above family tree; they all start from Osewe Ko-Char, Osewe had three wives. The first wife is Ojode (Colunm 1) she is the mother of Oyuga and Okong'o, whose current offspring is Otieno Ogonda and Osewe Ojode (Coulum 1). The second wife is Abonyo, the mother of Mbawi, the current offspring are Opere Oiko and Harun Ouro. Osewe's third wife is my great grandmother known as Muche she bore two sons and these are Robi and Nyauchi. Robi is the father of Nayawanga (Kingi) and Nyandwa. The families that occupy Kunya Kosewe belong to three brothers these are Nyawanga and Ogundo I have not ignored any relative I have merely taken the ones that were available during the validation workshop. The Osewe clan belong to the Kabudha clan, Osewe is the son of Ochar, Ochar is the son of Otonde, Otonde is the son of Were, Were is the son of Ocharo and Ocharo is the son of Ojal. Ojal is the grandfather of Jo-Kabudha, Ojal is the brother of Onege, their mother is known as Amolo the daughter of Le (Amolo Nyar Le). The Household of Owilla, his Offsprings and present clans is drawn here below. Owilla had four wives, the four wives come from two families and these are the Nyiywen and Le. The first wife is Ng'o the daughter of Nyiywen, they form the Kobong' clan. The second wife is Amolo the daughter of Le, they form the Kabudha and katweng'a clan. The third wife is Adeka they form the Kokwiri clan and Jo-Karateng' of Kisumu Karateng'. The fourth wife is Gori the daughter of Nyiywen, she is the sister of the first wife Ngo' her off-springs are Otwal who also form Jo-Kobong'

OWILA'S OFFSPRINGS

The Owila family is drawn here-below based on the wives, According to Luo culture, it is the women who form the house holds. The Home is headed by a man, he is the Chairman as would be in the modern Company managerial organizational structure, and the woman would be refered to as the Managing Director. The myth that Owila is the father of Jo-Uyoma is false, l would rather refer to him as the patriarch of Uyoma.

Just like Ramogi ll and Jok are not the grandfather of the Luo as imagined, and professor Ogot refers to them as mytical figures, but for me l refer to them as patriarchs. In regard to Owila, his house hold and offsprings are clearly known and drawn here below.

	WIVES/HOUSEHOLDS	OFFSPRINGS	PRESENT CLANS	PRESENT LOCATION
1	Ng'o the daughter of Nyiywen	Omolo Ngo'ng'o Okelo	Kobong'	Central Uyoma
2	Amolo the daughter of Le (Amolo Nyar Le)	Ojal	Kabudha	South/East and Central Uyoma
		Onege	Katwenga'	South/East and Central Uyoma
3	Adeka the daughter of Le (Adeka Nyar Le)	Liech	Died before marriage	
		Owuor	Assimilated by Kokwiri	West Uyoma
		Okwiri	Kokwiri	West Uyoma
		Rateng'	Karateng' of Kisumu Karateng	Kisumu District
4	Goi/Goi the daughter of Nyinywen (Sister of Ngo')	Otwal	Kobong'	Central Uyoma

Now it may sound boring but you will be amazed to learn that the Somali Community are taught the family tree from the time they join *Madras* at between the age of five years and ten years. It is easy for the Somali to recite their family tree to the tenth generation. My friend Abdi Somo told me that he was able to recite his family tree beyond the tenth generation by the time he was 12 years old. This teaching is today missing in our upbringing and that is why we lose our identity. Just a few people in Uyoma can recite their geneaological background up like Oyuga Nyauchi, Aete Samba, Apolo Washington Juma, Odongo Nyandwa and Sombe Nyawanda, Odeny Ngure and Ogola Okendo among others, they were the only ones who could recite the family tree up to the 11th or 12th generation which is Owila.

Imagine you went to China and you lost your passport near the Great Wall of China and you find yourself without a passport, you will not be able to identify yourself, you will be arrested for being in China illegally, then you will be very lost. This book is written as an eye opener and to challenge you to find your root in this maze the way I have done. Do those relatives in Kisumu Karateng know that their origin is Uyoma? What about Kawango, what about Kanyamwa. What about you. Now if you are truly Ja-Uyoma please trace your family tree in this maze.

UYOMA FAMILY AND CLAN TREE

	JO-KABUDHA				JO-KATWENGA		JO-KOBONG'		JO-KOKIRI		ASEMBO
1	LWANDE	OWENDA	OGOLA	ODANDE	OMOLO	OTITO	ODIE	ODENY	OPONDO	ODOYO	Xx
2	Oneko	Onyango	xx	Odande	Owi	Yongo	Xx	Odeny 2	Xx	xx	Otiato (ogaja)
3	Achieng Oneko	Otieno	Ogola	Ogweny	Rayuayi	Otito	Xx	Oulo	Opondo	Ochiel	Opanga
4	Oneko Nyauchi	Owenda	Okendo	Odande	Amolo	Yongo	Odie	Ngure 2	Okong'o	Adhola	ALuoch
5	Nyauchi	Odalo	Oyuga	Okong'o	Ramburo	Obayo	Ngure	Odeny	Oswago	Oluoch	Okoth
6	Osewe	Ojwang	Bake	Ogweny	Nyasio	Oluga	Ofire	Ngure	Okweso	Obuyai	Omolo
7	Ochar	Andhoga	Ochar	Ogundo	Yongo	Orwa	Ojwang'	Oulo	Midega	Milai	Oremo
8	Otonde	Otieno	Ocharo	Otonde	Owade	Oluoch	Migot	Nyakinya	Moi	Obor	Njiri
9	Were	Odiembo	Were	Were	Odero	Okuma	Olang'	Jeje	Midega	Okwiri	Otumba
10	Ocharo	Otieno	Ocharo	Ocharo	Monye	Monye	Kisino	Kisino	Owuor	Ochieng	Onyango
11	Ojal	Ojal	Ojal	Ojal	Onege	Onege	Otwal	Otwal	Okwiri	Ajore	Owuor
12	Owila	Owila	Owila	Owila	Owila	Owila	Owila	Owila	Owila	Dilang'	Dilang
13	Odhiriany										
14	Omia Ramul										
15	Ramogi lll										

From Omia ramul then goes to Luo as indicated below

Ramogi lll (Jadolo) –the son of Oywa/Nyaluo –son of Ramogi ll (Ajwang') –son of Podho ll – son of Ramogi l (Olum) –son of Jok ll – son of Nayo – son Jok l – son of Twaifo – son of Owat –son of Ringrok – son of Podho l –son of Sinakuru –son of Luo

THE OWILA EXODUS AND SETTLEMENT

The introduction to the Owila exodus will lead us to the History and story of Uyoma Heroes and Gladiators, this introduction captures the summary of the detailed narration of this book. This book traces the History and story of Jo-Uyoma Heroes and Gladiators starts from Samia, then to Got Ramogi. After Got Ramogi the exodus takes us to Thurmony, Kawango, Kanyamwa and back to Thurmony. Thurmony is the central point of the present Uyoma Location. The Central point originally known as Thurmony is the present Madiany centre, the headquarters of Uyoma. Thurmony or Madiany is the burial site of Omia Ramul and Owila who can be referred to as the Uyoma Patriarchs. This burial site remains the Historical Uyoma Ancestral land Owila remains the undisputed Uyoma historical patriarch. All the people living in Uyoma are known as the grandchildren of Owila, *Nyikwa Owila*, this is regardless of whether you settled there Yesterday, Today or Tomorrow.

The diagram below shows the exodus of the Owila movement and settlement called the Owila exodus and settlement. The history of Jo-Uyoma in this book starts from Samia and finally culminates in the present Uyoma geographical and administrative location. Below here is the diagram of the Owila settlement from and tos Thurmony – Madiany.

THE OWILA EXODUS AND SETTLEMENT

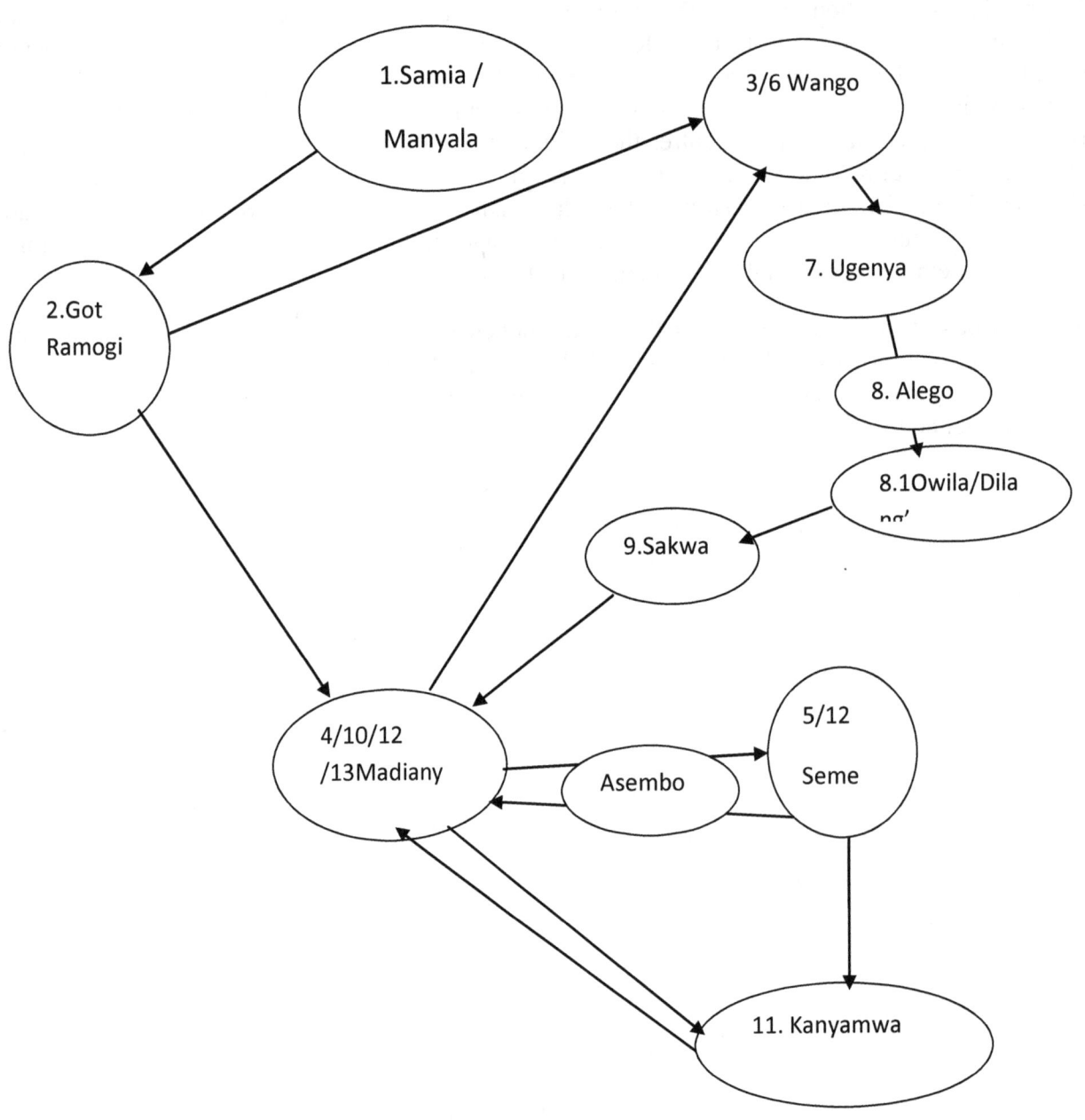

The diagram above shows the exodus of the Uyoma family from no.1 showing Samia to the present Uyoma showing no.13. The numbering is giving the places where they settled and moved again until the present day, the numbering includes an explanation of the places and their names as shown here below under summary of Uyoma exodus.

SUMMARY OF OWILA EXODUS AND SETTLEMENT

1. Movement of Ramogi Ajuang' from Samia to Got Ramogi as a young warrior.
2. Ramogi Ajuang' settles at Got Ramogi, in Yimbo Kadimo.
3. Wango the second son of Ramogi was the first to move from Got Ramogi to Kawango
4. Omia Ramul, Chwanya, Nyikal and Rado move from Got Ramogi.
   Omia Ramul settles in Thurmony (Uyoma), while Chwanya moved to Uyoma and then to Kanyamwa up to date. Rado and Nyikal move to Seme through Uyoma and Asembo.
5. Rado and Nyikal move to Seme and settle there to date
6. Dilang' and Owila the sons of Odhiriany and grandsons of Omia Ramul move from Uyoma to settle in Kawango for a short span of time, two to three generations.
7. Jo-Uyoma through Ugenya
8. From Owila's descendants (Jo-Uyoma) move from Kawango through Ugenya and settles in Alego Kobare at *Gunda Uyoma* in Uyoma village where the present Uyoma Primary/Secondary schools School near Rang'ala Secondary Schools are located.
8.1 Part of Dilang's family move to Asembo to form Omia Mwalo, Omia Diere and Omia Malo
9. Jo-Uyoma move from Alego past Gem into Sakwa, then Asembo towards Uyoma
10. Jo-Uyoma move to Uyoma and settle for less than a generation
11. Jo-Uyoma move to Kanyamwa
12. This number appears twice, one, Part of Jo-Uyoma move from Kanyamwa to Uyoma through Seme and Asembo on one direction, two, the other part of Jo-Uyoma move from Kanyamwa straight to Uyoma on the other direction
13. Jo-Uyoma settles in Uyoma up to today. That was the end of the Exodus in the Uyoma ancestral land.
    So where I am settled in Kunya is the true ancestral land of Jo-Uyoma where the umbilical cords have been buried and will be buried for ever and ever.
    It is important to note that Luo land is demarketed by burial sites of the heads of Homes and the umbilical cord signifies land ownership like tittle deeds.

THE MAP SHOWING THE UYOMA EXODUS AND SETTLEMNET

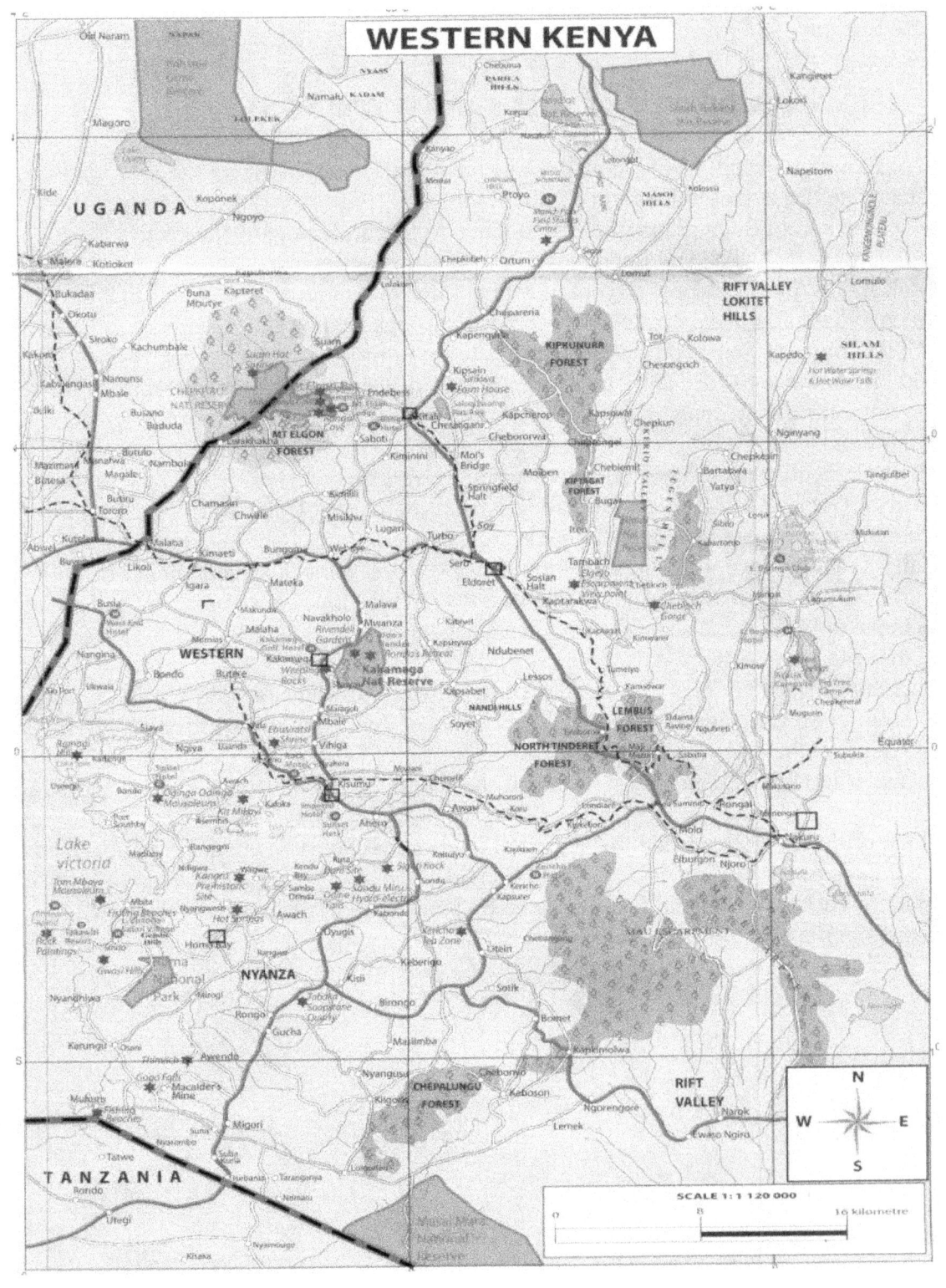

THE UYOMA EXODUS

The Uyoma movement known as the Owila exodus starts with the migration of his grandfather Ramogi Ajuang' (II) from the present Samia area to Got Ramogi in present Yimbo to the present Uyoma after various expeditions through the current Siaya County to the present Kakamega County, back to Siaya County across the present Lake Victoria to Homa Bay County and back to Siaya County. The exodus entailed navigating the land and water terrain in search for land for settlement and coexistence with friendly neighbourhood.

In this book we will be talking of exodus, journey and movements, it is important to note that these were not high speed movements. Usually hunters from one group would survey the new found land and if they found it suitable for settlement they would convince their relatives to move to the new found land. Therefore these movements, journeys and exodus would take months and years considering the fact that most of the people during those years were very migratory in search of *fish'as the joke goes the Luos follow the Nile in search of fish and chips'*.

THE MOVEMENT FROM GOT RAMOGI

Ramogi Ajwang' (II) is the the son of Oywa and was born in Bunyala, this is where part of the Luo, the Jii speaking group settled and built their home (Ligala) after their movement from the present Uganda after having lived there among the Busoga. This group of Luo is known as the Jii-speakers according to Professor William.R.Ochieng of Maseno University in his book on the history of Egypt and the Nile Valley from Ancient times.

The Luos in Kenya are divided into four expansionist divisions, this include Joka-Jok , Joka-Owiny, Joka – Omolo and those who allied themselves with the Suba .Their evolution and spread into Kenya 's Lake region from Northern Uganda took place over very long period of time. Joka-Jok is the first group of Luos to arrive in Kenya and specifically Nyanza between 1490 and 1517, Owila of Uyoma is the descendant of Joka-Jok. The second group of Luos is Joka-Owiny who arrived in Nyanza between A.D. 1530 and 1630. This group moved from Budoola camps in Eastern Uganda to Western Alego, the group includes clans such as Kaugagi, Mur and Nyala and assimilated non-Luo group such as Karapul and Kanyaboli. They were led by Owiny brother of Adhola of the Padhola in Uganda. The third group who are Jo-Komolo arrived in Nyanza between A,D. 1540 to 1640. They include Jo-Ugenya, Jo-Kakan in present Alego, Jo-Kadet in Gem; the Umuri, Urwana, Udongo and Umanya in Samia; the Kakan, Kanyada and Kochia in Southern Nyanza. Ugenya and Ragem were brothers whose father was Ochielo from the Pawir Kingdom; they left Pakwach-Pawir area in Uganda and headed to Western Kenya.

During this period when the Luos were moving into Nyanza in the present Kenya, the Maasai were living and roaming around Nyakach with their cattle.The Nandi people were living around Kisian. The Maragoli and their kinsmen the Abagusii were living between Kisumu and Yimbo in a nomadic life style.

As the Luo population grew they started edging out these other tribes from the lake shore settlement for fish, water and pasture. Even though the Luos would fight against each other, it was common for them to team together whenever none Luo attacked any of their kinsmen.

The Luo settlement in the present Nyanza and around Winam Gulf can reasonably be said to have taken place between A.D. 1490 and 1790.

Ramogi Ajwang' (II) a young and energetic warrior led the Joka-Jok descendants group of Luos from the present Bunyala and settled at Got Ramogi, the present Yimbo in Bondo, Siaya County. Ramogi Ajuang' had offsprings who included Third Jok, Ramogi Jadolo (III), Omia and Wango were from the same mother, she is known as Aloo Nyar Omulo. Jok begot Nyasgenga who form Wajare of Kisii. The second son of Jok is Chwanya who presently form the Kanyamwa, Kadem, Karungu and Kabuoch. The five clans of Chwanya are known as Joka-Onyango Rabala.The third sson of Jok is Omwa who migrated to the present Kisumu Karateng'. The fourth was Rachuonyo who is the patriarch of Karachuonyo and Kasipul Kabondo.

The descendants of Omia Ramul the son of Ramogi Ajuang' are the present Jo-Uyoma and the Jo-Kowuor, Jo-Kokise, Jo-Konyango and Joka-Malumbe of the Eastern Asembo.

Wango of the present Kawango moved to the Eastern side at Wuoroya or River Lisimu in Butere in Western Kenya, Kakamega County.Wango and Omia Ramul were first cousins to Matar, he is the Sakwa patriarch.

Due to internal sibling rivalries, population growth and in search of greener pastures the Ramogi family decided to separate and move to different directions *Dar e kwe dak* (Family separation creates harmony) This is a situation when part of the family move out to another place to create space, or preference for some other geographical area.

The movements were as follows:

SETTLEMENT OF DIMO

Dimo is the son of Ramogi Jadolo (III) being the eldest sibling remained in his father's home. The Dimo descendants are the present Yimbo Kadimo people occupying the South Western part of the Bondo District in Siaya County in Luo Nyanza.From the second wife Dimo begot Rado and Nyikal who peresntly occupy Seme of Kisumu County.

The settlement of some of the present Yimbo people which is currently in Bondo District in Siaya County was led by Dimo the son of Ramogi Jadolo (III). The group includes Joka-Dimo, Joka-Munyenjra,-Joka-Owili

MOVEMENT OF WANGO

Wango and his family was the first group that left Got Ramogi, they headed towards the North-Eastern *Masawa-Wuok chieng'* side of Got Ramogi to Aora Wuoroya (*River Nzoia*) the present Butere Mumias District in Kakamega County. The Wango family has settled in this place to date, they formed the Kawango Kingdom; these are the descendants of Mumia Nabongo. When they settled in the present Mumias they met, intermarried and lived with the Bantu groups and they started mixing the Luo language with Bantu and today they do not speak Luo language as we know it. The movement and settlement of Kawango people who currently occupy Butere and Mumias Districts in Kakamega County was led by Wango the son of Ramogi Ajwang'(II), he is the brother of Omia Ramul from the same mother. Matar the patriarch the Grandfather of Sakwa people moved to the southern part of Mumias and started a family in Alego and then moved with his offspring to the present Sakwa Bondo Sub-County. Matar was the son of Wango the brother of Omia Ramul hence the blood relationship between the Sakwa and Kawango people and Jo-Uyoma.

THE MOVEMENT OF THE OTHER SIBLINGS

Omia Ramul and his other siblings; Chwanya, Rado and Nyikal took the movement towards the Southern *Milambo* part of Got Ramogi. The rugged and distressful journey took them to higher altitude/contour *Thurmony* the present Madiany in Uyoma next Got Naya.

This journey was led by Omia Ramul the son of Ramogi Ajwang' (II).

This is the modern Likungu Beach in West Uyoma, it is the entry point into Uyoma of Omia Ramul and his siblings from Got Ramogi in Yimbo.

MOVEMENT OF CHWANYA

Omia Ramul, Chwanya, Nyikal and Rado moved from Got Ramogi, they entered the present Uyoma through Likungu Beach in West Uyoma and they all temporarily settled there. After a short span of time and in order to keep cordial relationship among the siblings they decided to separate company. Chwanya moved across the shallow waters of Nam Lolwe the current Lake Victoria or the Nyanza Gulf. Chwanya settled with his clan in the current Kanyamwa. Today the Chwanya clan is settled in Kanyamwa and some of the offsprings can today be found in other areas such as Kabwoch, Karungu and Kadem, which they colonized. This is the area where you will find the Historical site known as *Thim Lich Ohinga*.

The movement from Thurmony by the Jo-Kanyamwa in Homa Bay County was led by Chwanya the son of Jok. During those days the strip between Uyoma and Kanyada was wadeable, *inyalo yor gi tielo*.

MOVEMENT OF RADO AND NYIKAL

Since Nyikal and Rado were maternal brothers they decided to move together towards the North Eastern *Wuok Chieng' massawa* side of Thurmony *Madiany* through Asembo and settled in the present Seme District of Kisumu County. In this exodus, Rado took with him a big population of Kasmori people who were living in the present Kayundi and Kakremba in the present Uyoma. The Rado people includes the following clans; Kolunje, Koker and Kaila in Seme. The Nyikal people include the following clans; Kadipir, Kadinga, Kowe, Kakelo and Kombija of Seme in Kisumu County.

The movement from Thurmony by the Seme people who currently occupy Seme District, Kisumu County was led by Rado.

THE EXODUS OF UYOMA BY OMIA RAMUL

Omia Ramul and his family moved from Got Ramogi through Sakwa to Thurmony *Madiany* and stayed there for a short period of time. The leader in this movement was Omia Ramul the son of Ramogi Ajwang' (II).

Omia Ramul had one son called Odhiriany. Odhiriany married Otimbla *nyar kobunga* then Dilang' and Owila were born. Omia Ramul died and was buried in the present Madiany infront of Madiany Primary School gate. This burial site marks the significance of Thurmony, the present Madiany as the Uyoma ancestral cradle land, and hence the Uyoma ancestral land. Dilang' got married while in Thurmony, by this time the legendary Owila was still young and single.

The family of Omia Ramul, Led by Odhiriany moved to Wuoroya-Kawango through Sakwa, Alego and Ugenya. Their movement was as a result of famine, hostility of the original inhabitants of present Uyoma; Jokobunga and Jowagoro, coupled with inadequate grazing land and access to water points. They lived in Kawango for a period equivalent to two to three generations by this time their kin of Wango origin spoke Luo language with Bantu *Luhya* dominated accent, these were the present Maragoli.

The movement from Thurmony to Kawango was led by Dilang' the first son of Odhiriany, Owila is his younger brother.

THE GENESIS OF UYOMA

While on their way to Kawango, Owila met Ng'o and Gori daughters of Nyiywen of Alego and Amolo and Adeka of Kale as his four wives. Dilang' and Owila the sons of Odhiriany settled with their Siblings along River Lisimu/Wuoroya the present River Nzoia. The Luos call it Wuoroya and the Luhyias call it Lisimu. During their stay in Kawango Owila offspring's already formed the core foundation of the Uyoma family as we know it today but at that time it was simply the Owila nuclears family. Owila therefore is the patriarch of Jo-Uyoma, after the death of his brother Dilang' in Kawango.

When Dilang's and Owilas were in Kawango, they were refered to as the Omia *Jokomia* the name of their grandfather, Omia Ramul. Who was the brother of Wango. During their stay in Kawango, they occupied the present Mumias sugar factory compound. The name Mumias is derived from Omia because the homestead used to be refered to as the Omia.

The Omia Ramul descendants especially in the lineage of Dilang' have retained the name of Omia Ramul. They occupied Omia Mwalo, Omia Diere and Omia Malo of Eastern Asembo of Rarieda sub-county. The Dilang's offspring in Uyoma are Jokajore, the offsprings Ajore's first wife, *Lur*.

OWILA'S OFFSPRINGS

	WIVES/HOUSEHOLDS	OFFSPRINGS	PRESENT CLANS	PRESENT LOCATION
1	Ng'o the daughter of Nyiywen	Omolo Ngo'ng'o Okelo	Kobong'	Central Uyoma
2	Amolo the daughter of Le (Amolo Nyar Le)	Ojal Onege	Kabudha (Odero) Katwenga'	South/East and Central Uyoma South/East and Central Uyoma
3	Adeka the daughter of Le (Adeka Nyar Le) (Sister of Amolo)	Liech Owuor Okwiri Rateng'	Died before marriage Assimilated by Kokwiri Kokwiri Karateng' of Kisumu Karateng	West Uyoma West Uyoma Kisumu District
4	Gori the daughter of Nyiywen (Sister of Ngo')	Otwal	Kobong'	Central Uyoma

Adeka was inherited upon the death of Owila by Ochieng' Opuk Laro the son of Ajore, the grandson of Dilang' the brother of Owila.

Adeka moved temporarily and or eloped *opor* to Kisumu and gave birth to Rateng, They are the Jo-Karateng' of Kisumu. She later returned (*Odhi oduogo*) to Uyoma in her marital home where she was buried; in the modern Luo terminology she would be called (*Ogo kam bak*).

THE NUISANCE OF OMOLO NG'ONGO (Omolo Ng'ongo)

The genesis of the name Uyoma was coined at the time Jo-Uyoma lived in Kawango. Jo-Uyoma lived in Kawango at the site of the current Mumias Sugar Factory in Mumias, the name of the area Mumias originates from the name Omia Ramul the Uyoma Patriarch. In some Luhya dilect it would be something to this effect *Yiri ni ridara ria Mumia*, In Luo it would be *Ma en dala Jo-Komia*.

Adjacent to the Mumias Sugar factory, there is a compound that has been left undisturbed as a preserve of Jo-Omia Ramul who are today Jo-Uyoma and part of Asembo. It is alledged that it is a bad omen for anyone to plough or settle on that piece of land, just like Gunda uyoma in Alego Kobare.

Stories has it that one white ma who thought he was brave dared to clear and plough the land in Mumias using a tractor. As he went about his ploughing, a serpant appeared from no where at bit him on the head, he fell and died instantly, his tractor was grounded there for months and all the efforts to repair it failed, it had to be pulled from there using other means, the man who had been warned by the natives served as an example to anyone who had interest in that piece of land.

There were many sibling squabbles and hence the departure of Jo-Uyoma, but the main one was triggered by Omolo Ng'ong'o.

Omolo Ngo'ngo' was the first son of Owila and his wife Ngo' Nyar Nyiwen. Omolo was a hyper active destructive child and comical and yet result oriented. Some times he was refered to as *Omolo Ng'ongo to en Ja oyuma* (Omolo is senior in regard to lineage but he is comical and loves jokes). When Omolo came of age he would take the calves for grazing with the other younger siblings. He always took charge and command of the boys of his family being the permanent team leader. He soon learnt to break the oxen and train them to plough. He taught his brothers how to milk effectively with high production. While grazing he would train his young male siblings fighting techniques and skilled wrestlling, swimming, fishing and hunting. Omolo was the terror of the village. He terrorized boys from other clans and by the end of the day the Owila and Dilang' family were well guarded. Even the night runners *Jo juogi* would not dare to step in their homes. The family was very fond of Omolo but Owila was extremely supportive of his son's activities which in some areas seemed to have positive returns to the family. He later took full charge of ploughing with the bulls and set the boys to weed the fields.

The game the children played in Kawango at the River Wuoroya is similar to an incident that I personaly witnessed in Kunya at Oneko beach in the orchad in 1958. The game imitates crocodiles killing technic, it entails holding somebody under the water and other children would count the length of time you would hold your breath under the water. It was also used as a swimming training. In my case and my other sibling, it was unfortunate that as we were playing a crocodile was keenly watching us and getting ready to attack us. I was third in breath holding, when the fifth person went under the water the crocodile burst out of its hiding place, bashed the standing children, crabbed Orwa under the water and we never saw him again until today. The mother cried like a mother, I will never forget this incident, because I only looked for my mother and I could not speak for one week.

Some of the older boys among us behaved like Omolo Ng'ongo and we had to learn how to swim and improve breath holding under the water. My own uncle Ogare Oneko was extremely fond of this game and many children were hurt in the process. This game is no good at all but it is a growing up harzard if you are an Uyoma boy born in Uyoma, during grazing. Uyoma is surrounded by water, it is water every where therefore you must learn how to swim.

Back to Kawango One bad incident occurred during their herding; Omolo in his usual bullying spree, he pushed a Kawango boy into the river and the boy suffered minor injuries. The Kawango clan called on the Owila clan so that the issue could be addressed. The Owila clan brushed them aside and said that they could not sit to discuss childish games or silly jokes from children *Weche nyithindo mag oyuma*. At this point Owila was the family leader, was notoriously rude and thurgish. The Kawango clan elders were very unhappy and disappointed. The Owila family used the word *oyuma* several times, until Kawango clan nicknamed them *Abayuma* (The people of jokes).The Kawango clan wrongly pronounced Oyuma as Uyoma and the Owila ridiculously echoed their way of poor pronounciation, a habit that ended up establishing the name as Uyoma.

The second time that the swimming saga took place, was when one of the Kawango boys who could not swim as well as the Owila boys actually drowned and died after being carried home by Omolo and his colleagues. This time the whole clan of the Kawango people took stern stand with the Owila family and their Dilang brethrens. The first step was that they the families were barred from attending the funeral before the issue was settled. The Dilang' family supported the Owila family and agreed that they would not attend the meeting to discuss children affairs *Weche nyithindo mag oyuma* even at the face of death. Later the Kawango family gave Owila and Dilang family an ultimatum to move out of Kawango. In his usual arrogance Owila told the Kawango clan I have our home *An gi thurwa*. Owila was ailing at this time due to age but was strong enough to address his family. He called a meeting of the whole clan (Dilang's and Owila's family). He addressed the clan advising them to return to their ancestral land (Thurmony). He concluded his speech by saying " East or West Home is best' *Thuro lo yiengo' wadoguru Thurwa.Jogo owe chando uka*. Incidentally it is recorded that Dilang' and Owila were different characters, Dilang was known as a peace lover and negotiator, but like all the Omia Ramul descendants battle was not foreign and he spent most of his time training his siblings on war skills. Owila incidentally was a man who was extremely a war like brute who would dare battle any day or night, he would literally provoke even minor fights. He was rude, arrogant, and fierce and encouraged conflict all the time. When Dilang was still alive he would tame his younger brother Owila and their life in Kawango was peaceful and amicable. After Dilang's death Owila took over and sibling conflict started between Jo-Kawango and Jo-Uyoma and the relationship started deteriorating.The worst thing is that Owila started cattle raiding among their neighbours without Jo-Kawango's knowledge. The wealthier he became the more arrogant he became and he created poor relationship between Jo-Kawango and their neighbours.

At this time Owila's elder brother Dilang had already passed away and Owila was now Jo Uyoma patriarch incharge of the family according to Luo tradition. Owila exodus started soon after the funeral of the Kawango boy which they had snubbed to the surprise of the Kawango people. This is because during funerals according to Luo tradition families should put aside their quarrels, attend to the funeral and then discuss other issues later. This negative gesture created long term bad blood between the two blood brothers that is Omia Ramul and the Wango siblings. The Owila family ignored, snubbed the funeral ceremony and the Kawango plight. In the meantime Omolo Ngo'ngo had escaped for fear of his life. He resurfaced during the movement to Alego. As Owila's eldest son, Omolo was pampered by his family and entire clan who viewed him as the pillar: *wuoyi siro* despite his mischievous behavior, they reasoned that he was the elder one no matter how bad he was *Omolo the elder one i.e Omolo Ngo'ngo ong'ino ok ma ng'wende*. The Wango clan due to their diluted Luo could not pronounce the ng'ongo properly hence *Omolo Ng'ong'o*. The word *joyuma* was pronounced by the Wango people as Abayuma and hence the name Uyoma from the sentence Jo-Oyuma. Until the recent past Juo-Uyoma do not intermarry and similarly the relationship between Wango and Omia ramul who were siblings from the same mother Aloo nyar omulo and ramogi jadolo were not supposed to intermarry until the recent past.

OMIA OFFSPRINGS EXITS FROM KAWANGO

They left Kawango due to these domestic misunderstandings with their brethrens. Their expedition covered Ugenya, and then they temporarily settled in Alego near Rang'ala in a village known todate as Uyoma village where the present Uyoma Primary and Secondary Schools in Alego Kobare are located, the place is known as Gunda Uyoma.

GUNDA UYOMA

Owila moved his clan to the present Alego Kobare and decided to settle there temporarily while waiting to return to Thurmony the Omia Ramul ancestral land. Since they moved from Kawango in haste Owila had to carry out research on the entry back to the current Uyoma. While in Alego Kobare many clan rerseachers were sent to Thurmony on fact finding missions to ensure soft landing back home.

The first step to ensure security in Alego was to shield out the neighbours that were not friendly. The first unfriendly neighbors were Jo-Ugenya Kager; they were viewed as unfriendly because Jo-Kawango were very friendly to them. Owila pitched battle with Jo-Kager at the present Uyoma Primary School and Secondary School. They forcefully evicted them from their homes, killed them, burnt their houses and drove them more than thirty kilometers from the boundary. Owila was sure that Jo-Kawango would not dare to fight after a mammoth defeat of Jo-Kager. Owila gladiators came home with herds of livestock, women and children. Any revenge would come after a long time in the future by which time Owila estimated that he would have driven his clan to Uyoma.

The author standing in the trench that was dug around Gunda Uyoma. The left side is the outer while the inner side is on the right

The second unfriendly neighbours were the Kalenjin known as *kombekombe* who were notorious for night cattle raiding. Owila decided to give them a taste of their own medicine. Owila attacked the

Kalenjin at night and raided their cattle in hundreds. Owila waited for one week and then he attacked the Kalenjin unaware during the day from early morning. It was not a fight but a massacre; hundreds of Kalenjins were killed, the remaining livestock taken plus women and children. The evidence of battle remained in the area with scattrered skulls which were seen in the 1950s by many people who are still alive today in Alego.

Owila trained his gladiators that during any battle, property must be looted and women must be taken captive to increase the population. The increased population ensured labour force to ensure food security. The women would also produce more men to become warriors to enhance military supremacy. Owila's philosophy was never to kill women and children, this is the back bone of any given society and so Owila ensured that no women or children were molested, they were always protected.

The third step was to build a secure home for his clan. He shielded the neighbours and settled on a more than twenty kilometer radius. This area covered the following current geographical sites, Uyoma Gul, Uyoma Bar, Uyoma Nyakonja and Uyoma Rachwi. It stretched to the area today known as Uyoma Kobare. This large land was demarcated by Owila for food production and grazing. The whole area was jealously guarded and any intruder would face the wrath of Owila and his notorious gladiators who roamed the protected area.

The Owila homestead or village covered approximately more than twenty acres with a population of a thousand plus inhabitants. The home was surrounded by a deep and wide trench, it is estimated that the depth of the trench was 10 metres and the width was 8 metres. The soil was carefully hipped on the inside and hence climbing into the homestead was extremely difficult. Thorny trees were planted inside the home, this thorny tree known as *Ooyo* was used to protect intruders, it also had magical and has sports values. The home had about four gates; these gates were jealously guarded by the gladiators both day and night. River Nyamboyo which connects with Wuoroya was located infront of the gates for livestock water points and for drawing domestic water, these drinking water points were known as Yao *owila*. The other rivers that surrounded the area are Huludhi and Hudundu. Matar later joined Jo-Kowila and settled on the opposite side across river Nyamboyo. We are informed that the trenches around the Owila homestead could not be climbed and as such, when our informant was twelve years old, if he jumped into the trench sorrounding the Owila compound, he had to use a ladder to get out of the trench from the outer part, but it was impossible for him to climb on the inner part. Today, the trench around the gunda is still visible and this is over 300 years ago. The notorious Owila knew that security was number one in human life. Some people say that since he was a terror, he knew that he had very many enemies and therefore he took security as an important part of his life. The site of the homestead is still evident and nobody has built a home in that abandoned home *Gunda*. According to Luo tradition it is wrong to build a home on a *Gunda*. Soil from the tench was hipped on the inner side and thorny trees were planted

Owila left a legacy of terror in Alego, Ugenya and Gem. He is negatively remembered for his notorious uncalled for raids of the the neighbours. Many neighbours hated the Owila clan with a passion.

The Owila actually overstayed in Alego due to research, planning and preparation for gand match to Thurmony. Even though they had settled in Alego, Owila insisted that the clan must go back to the chosen ancestral land by Omia Ramul. Other reasons included abundant grazing land, fertile land, access to fish and the security of the land surrounded by water in the shape of an onion with a narrow outlet to the current Asembo and Sakwa.

After living in Alego for about fifteen years, Owila was now very old and fragile due to age. In the company of his sons they climbed to the summit of Mt. Mwer (the present Got Ngi'ya in Alego. At the height of Got Ngi'ya one could see Got Naya and other places because the contour was very high. At this stage Owila pointed at Got Naya and exclaimed that is your home the land of your ancestors, where your great grandfather Omia Ramul was buried *Macha e thuru lop kwaru, kendo kama ne oikie Omia Ramul wuod Ramogi Ajwang'* (II)! This was his last gesture to his clan; plans were already underway for Uyoma exodus.

Showing the clan their home in Uyoma was Owila's first assignment, the second assignment was that when he dies they should bury him in Alego, move on and carry his grave stone *kit liende* to his ancestral land in Thurmony and then bury the stone on top of Got Naya as a symbol of identity of the ancestral land (Equivalent to the modern title deed). The grave stone will mark the Ancestral land which you must defend and keep for future posperity of the future generation.

It is recorded that Owila died in the first week of April 1730 A.D in Alego and was buried according to Luo traditions; they had stayed here for approximately fifteen years. After performing all the burial rites such as appeasing the spirits *tero buru* and dispersing of the mourners keyo *nyinyo* they continued their return match to *Thurmony* the ancestral land. The stories portrayed Owila people *Jo-Uyoma* as arrogant warriors who could easily conquer them and turn them into slaves. At this point while leaving Alego part of Dilang's family split to the current Asembo they today form the Jo-Komia consisting of Jokise, Kowuor, Konyango, Kochola, Kamalumbe and Kayoo.This is the deep rooted blood relationship of Jo-Uyoma and Jo-Komia. The Jo-Kajore clan of Uyoma today are the ones who carried the Owila's gravestone and it should be noted that Jo-Kajore of Uyoma do not intermarry with Jo-Komia of Asembo and specifically Kowuor and Kokise. Tinda Ja-Kajore was the first to establish a home on behalf of Owila's family from Kawango, and then Owila's sons followed suit. The Kajore clan were the first to perform the rituals.

At this point all the Owila sons were married except Onege. Jo Uyoma decided that they could not migrate while Onege was single, they eloped with an Alego girl known as Atweng'a the daughter of Bwong' *Atwenga' Nyar Buong'* against the girl's parent's wish, this was at the eve of the migration. At the wee hours of that morning they forcefully migrated with Buong' who was following the trail of his daughter Atweng'a the newly married wife of Onege. Ajore is the one who carried the grave stone *kit liel* of Owila with him from Alego Kobare to Abom in Sakwa; this is where Ajore died and was buried. Tinda the son of Ajore took the mantle of carrying the gravestone from Abom to Thurmony in Uyoma.

When they were moving from Alego, the Uyoma warriors raided, looted and drove all the cattle with them from Matar's home. It is difficult to imagine that Owila actually raided Matar's home and yet Matar is his first cousin. Matar is Wango's offspring; Owila is Omia Ramul's offspring. Wango and Omia Ramul are brothers from the same mother. Some of the cattle they raided were handed over to Buong' the father of Atwenga' as dowry. Later they took refuge at Kale's home the son of Silwal. Mean while word spread that Jo-Uyoma had actually raided their kin and neighbour Jo-Sakwa, Matar's offsprings. Jo-Kawango organized to persue Jo-Uyoma, not to get away with this mischief. They grouped with Jo-Sakwa, Jo-Ugenya and Jo-Alego. They followed Jo-Uyoma for vengeance for all the havock they had caused when in Kawango and rude departure from Alego. The movement from Alego went across River Yala through Abom in Sakwa Ndira.

They settled temporaily in Abom at the present Abom Primary School. Ajore who was their leader died and was buried there. Otwal the son of Owila took over the leadership of the Jo-Uyoma towards the promised ancestral land in Thurmony.

Le the brother of Amolo the wife of Owila then helped Jo-Uyoma to escape the attack, he misdirected the Alego, Matar and Kawango warriors that their enemy Jo-Uyoma were headed towards the Western direction *Podho chieng'* and yet they were moving towards the Southern *Milambo* part of the region across river *Aora* Kauko. They lost trace of Jo-Uyoma but promised that if ever Jo-Uyoma attempted a come-back, all of them would re-group and fight them.

After moving from Abom they trekked across River Kauko near Got Rambugu in Asembo Kakia, then down through Kipasi and Anyuongi in Sakwa. Their expedition continued further through Lusi to Gwena. At this point one group moved to Nyabera and the other group headed through Pala Kobong' and settled in Thurmony the promised ancestral land.

Obong' was the son of Chwanya; Chwanya was the brother of Omia Ramul the grand father of Owila. Obong' was left behind in the present Uyoma when the Chwanya family moved to Kanyamwa. Obong' settled at Pala presently known as Pala Kobong'. The present land mark is Pala Kobong' Primary School.

When the Jo-Uyoma arrived in the present Uyoma they found that some of Jo- Sakwa, Jo-Kagwa, Jo-Kagan, Jo Kanyidoto,Jo Kopole, Jo-Kisumu,Jo-Wamiembe and remnants of Chwanya living in their ancestral land.

Otwal, Omolo and Okelo took their families, livestock and properties to Obong's home because Obong' was their first cousin. Ojal, Onege the Ajores and the Kokwiri (Owuor, Liech and Okiri) clans moved to Nyabera. Chwanya and Omia Ramul were brothers from Ramogi Jadolo (lll) and this was the relationship. This relationship is the rationale for Otwal, Omolo and Okelo in seeking refuge at Obong's home.

After various discussions it was agreed through Obong's suggestion and consensus that the three siblings should settle at Thurmony symbolically the burial site of Omia Ramul at the foot of Got Naya, which was their ancentral home that Owila had instructed them while in Alego while standing on top of Got Ng'iya (*ne osiemo negi thurgi kochung' ewi Got Ng'iya*) before his death.

The Gem *Kanyidoto* people resisted the entry of the Uyoma people to Thurmony it is at this point that a warrior called Chialo from Kokwiri clan and other warriors ganged up into the battle field against the Kanyidoto. The battle was only settled when Jo-Uyoma fell their ten warriors to the ground and crashed the rest of the fighters who were now fleeing in fear towards Okela field towards the great historical Nyamarimba. The Uyoma people did not pursue them any further, because their objective was to reach Thurmony, the promised site.

Tinda the son of Ajore is the one who carried the Owila grave stone. On the arrival at Thurmony the Uyoma warrior's equivalent to the gladiators led by Osike Kirina and Chialo surrounded the Thurmony environ to ensure that the enemy was subdued. The warriors regrouped chanting *(gweyo)* and imitating war dances *(Go-sira)*. The women met them dancing and ululating at the heroic entry into their promised ancestral land. The elders held one week burial ceremony. The grave stone was buried adjacent to Omia Ramul's Grave symbolically as the grave of Owila according to Luo traditons. It should be noted today that Owila's grave site is situated at the home of Mzee Peter Aete Samba behind Madiany District Hospital. The Grave of the head of a household is equivalent to the present title deed. and it is where decisions on land allocations are made.

After this great ceremony, the other clans of Jo-Uyoma moved towards different directions taking into consideration the land distribution amongst siblings according to seniority .Otimbla the mother of Owila was buried at dot age *ka oti ma imoyo amoya* Otimbla is the grandmother of Jo-Uyoma. The group that settled in the western and central parts of Uyoma includes the following families; Kotwal and Kokelo, Liech and Owuor. Kotwal, Komolo and Kokelo today forms the Obong' clan known as Jokobong' and they occupy the present Central Uyoma. Liech and Owuor today form the Kokwiri clan and they occupy Western part of Uyoma.

It should be noted that Okwiri was born out of wife inheritance by Ochieng' Opuk Laro the son of Ajore. Ajore was the son of Dilang' the elder brother of Owila, this justifies wife inheritance in the family or clan and hence the blood relationship. Incidentally the Liech and Owuor families have been assimilated under the Kokwiri umbrella, therefore they are known as Jo-Kokwiri.

The group that went to eastern and southern parts of thurmony was the Kabudha and Katwenga in relation to their household and land distribution traditions (*Jo-kamolo Nyar Silwal*)

THE TURBULANCES OF JO-UYOMA

The Bible says "What causes fights and quarrels among you. Don't they come from your desires that battle within you. You want something but don't get it' James 4;1;3
What was Jo-Uyoma looking for?
Was it just the Ancestral land?
Jo-Uyoma faced many challenges on their return from Kawango to their ancestral land, *Thurmony*. These challenges were brought about by the people who occupied the present Uyoma during their absence while they were living in Kawango. These *foreign* occupants included the following; Sakwa, Kagwa, Kasmori, Wamiembe, Wagoro, Kobunga, Kalir, Gem *Kanyidoto*, Kagan and Jo-Kisumu.

The Sakwa people people lived around Madiany, Rachar, Rimu, Lela Kasiri, Nyaguda and Gwena. The Asembo (Kale) people lived around Nyamasore, Ukunja, Ranalo, Rombo Moti and Kakremba. The Kagwa people lived around Ndere, Masala, Kayundi, Nyamasore, Matera and Manyuanda. The Kasmori people lived around Kakremba and Kogonga. The Wamiembe and Sigulu people lived around Naya and Lwanda Kotieno. The Wagoro people lived around Tanga and Wambisa. The Kobunga people lived around Nyakongo, Osindo and Ndhere. The Gem *Kanyidoto* people lived around Ragen'gni, Okela, Maramba, Lela, Kasiri and Kunya. The Kisumu people lived around Ruma and Kayundi. The dominating group of people living in the then Uyoma were Sakwa followed by Kagwa and Gem.

The remnants of these *foreign* occupants have remained in Uyoma and live peacefully with the house of Owila todate. Some have actually lost their identity while some maintained their identity, what is important is that today they are Jo-Uyoma and should never be refered to as foreigners otherwise everybody would be a foreigner in Uyoma.

On various occasions Jo-Uyoma would face unfriendly and unruly behavior from these Wagoro and Kobunga people. For instance when Jo-Uyoma drove their herd of cattle for watering toward the Western direction they were constantly obstructed by these foreign occupants hence the name Osindo. In Luo the word Osindo means denial or obstruction. Jo-Uyoma consulted various magicians to help dismantle these predicaments. The magician who came to their rescue was Osike Kirina the son of Oriwa from Kotwal of Kobong'. Osike Kirina carefully studied the Uyoma predicament which also touched and affected him being a member of the community. After meeting the Uyoma elders, he journeyed to an unknown place and reappeared several weeks later. In the heat of the night Osike Kirina summoned the Uyoma Elders and met at Thurmony at the grave site of Owila. The elders represented the following families Kajore, Kokelo, Kotwal, Kokwiri, Jokojal and Jokonege.

Here they slaughtered a black buck (*nyuok*) from the Kajore family and a white cock *Thuon gweno* was from Kokelo *Kobong'* family and the local brew busaa was provided by Jokojal Kabudha. These contributions were sacrifices offered to the ancestors and to appease the spirits. The meats were roasted on a bon fire and elders feasted upon them. They then sprinkled the local brew on the grave of their grandfather *Owila.* Finally each elder sipped the local brew and the magical concoction. He predicted that in the very near future you hear a ramble of two bull hippopotamus adjacent to the watering point, get ready to drive all your cattle and other livestock towards the watering point.

In the wee hours of a Saturday morning a loud rude noise filled the airwaves from Western direction and women of the village sent out a ululation sensing danger. On the same score the elders summed their sons to gather all the cattle and livestock and rode towards the Western direction to the water point as instructed by Osike Kirina. When they reached adjacent to the watering point they were amazed to find Osike Kirina waiting for them. He stopped them and he called the elders to watch the duel of the two hippos. The elders enjoyed themselves watching this great match, finally one hippo fell to ground. The foreigners were eagerly waiting for the duel to end so that they could slaughter the fallen hippo. When they were busy mass slaughtering the hippo and fighting over the meat Osike Kirina instructed Jo-Uyoma to drive their cattle to watering point. From that day Jo-Uyoma had access to this water point and named it *Osindo*, a name it bears to date.

Although Jo-Uyoma accessed the water point their troubles did not end, during the usual hot January season in the Uyoma peninsula scarcity of grass was very severe and one such season Jo-Uyoma ventured towards Eastern side of Madiany to graze their cattle. The grazing venture was cut short when they were faced by the Gem kanyidoto and Kopole foreigners. They hindered the young herdsmen from moving the valley with green pastures. The place is today known as *Rageng'ni* which can be translated into English as the point of hinderance.

MOVEMENT TO KANYAMWA

Jo-Uyoma faced many challenges ranging from hostility, cattle raiding, inadequate watering point, inadequate grazing space and famine. The day their children were hindered from grazing in the adjacent valley, the elders pondered on the next step of action. They held several consultative meetings and Obong' advised them to join their cousins in Kanyamwa where Chwanya clan had settled. Chwanya is the brother of Omia Ramul the grandfather of Owila hence the relationship.

The two groups lived in the present Uyoma for a period almost equivalent to one generation. Their settlement was short lived and they moved to Kanyamua, (the present Homa Bay County) following two distinct directions as advised by Osike Kirina the great Uyoma magician. The first group included the great magician Osike Kirina. They trekked on foot past Got Naya.

They crossed the shallow waters of Lake Victoria at Wikwang' point in South Uyoma to Kanyamwa. It is important to note that between Ndigwa in Uyoma and Got Huma, the area was not covered by the Nyanza Gulf waters as it is known today. The area was dominated by shallow waters and a few deep-points *nam ne thanythany*. This group was led by Midega Ralong'o, Otieno Auma and Mbuge Odeny. This group included two families; Kobong' and Kokwiri which is also known as Jokochamango'. Midega Ralong'o organized for boat rides across the lake. It is recorded that Ralong'o travelled looking backwards at Got Naya with tears rolling on his cheeks and at times swallowing the tears whenever the younger people looked at him. He swore that Jo-Uyoma will make a grand return to their ancestral land and he also blessed the *jokochamang'oni* to multiply while in the foreign land. He advised them to make sure that raid their neighbours livestock and women. The livestock will make them rich when they return to the ancestral land, the women will make them multiply and build strong armies, like Owila did when he was in Alego Kobare.

This is a drawing depicting one of the boats crossing to Kanyamwa. The man looking backwards is Midega Ralong'o. He is weeping about the Ancestral land

The second group took the current Asembo route into Seme through the present Ndere Island or Chula Rabuor and then to Kendu Bay. This route was covered by shallow waters that were wadable on foot except for a few deep points. This group was led by Abiero wuod Menya, Nyawanda, Onyango Otonde, Oguta and Opedhi. This group included the following families; Jokojal (*Kabudha*) Jokonege *Katwenga* Kajore, Kale *Asembo* and Kagwa.

It is important to take note that not ALL the families mentioned above went to Kanyamwa, remnants were left behind. These remnant families included Onimbo, Haya, Ogagla, Nyanyuma, Sigar and other families.

When Jo-Uyoma reached Kanyamwa, they were happily welcomed by their cousins from the Chwanya *The grandfather of Jo-Kanyamwa* who was the brother of Omia Ramul *The grandfather of Jo-Uyoma*. On arrival in Kanyamwa they found Kanyamwa surrounded by other clans such as Kabuoch, Karungu and Kadem. During the coming of Jo-Uyoma was the period of establishment in the region. There were several Bantu and Nilotic clans in the region at that time.

The Maasai grazed livestock around Kanyada all the way to Migori and beyond. The Asua were living in Karachuonyo, the Ugu lived in east Karungu and north Kadem, the Suna occupied Kadem and Wagire towards the Tanzanian boader. Then there were the notorious Jo-Wakabi the grandchildren of Wamlaji from Basoga in Uganda. They settled in Southern Nyanza earlier than the nilotes, they were few but very furious. One time they drove Kanyamwa all the way to Ligega and they constantly attacked Jo-Karungu. On the same score Kabuoch were also fierce and they moved the Maasai out of the zone. These neighours of Chwanya's offsprings were not very friendly and they kept on raiding each other. The evidence of the hostilities is the construction of the homes or villages as indicated and shown in the pictures of the village stone structures which were very security conscious. Apart from *Thim Lich Ohinga* there is evidence of 541 stone villages according to a researcher, Isaiah Onjala. The basic structure on the outer side is made of dry stone, while the innerside is a circular enclosure which is approximately four meters high and at least 15 meters diameter. Thim Lich Ohinga is today one of the Luo Historical sites. Here below are some of the pictures of Thim Lich Ohinga

The picture shows the main gate. It is built in such that the entrance is restricted and can be managed by the people inside the home.

This entry shows the great sense of security, similar to the trenches that Owila built while in Alego Kobare

The pictures above show the ruins that have managed the test of time. These have been rehabilitated by the Museums of Kenya

Thim Lich Ohinga was built in the 18th century on a hill, Thimlich Ohinga is a complex surrounded by stone walls now partially covered under Savannah bush land. The site consists of six enclosures and is a rare example of the first settlements in the region. Its stone wall is unique; it appears not to have had mortar applied originally and ranges from 1.2-4.2 meters in height and 1-3 meters in width. The walls surround the remnants of the once bustling urban center, now marked only by a series of house pits and cattle enclosures.

Although designated a national monument in 1981, several portions of the wall fell into disrepair. The main enclosure, for example, which measures about 140 meters diameter, lost several of its parts. Although all but one gate was blocked, the entire site was vulnerable to vandalism and trespassing. The conservation project was completed in two years.

Thimlich Ohinga is a rare, early example of defensive savanna architecture that led to this type of design becoming a traditional style across East Africa. It is a specimen of the stone walling practices and a communal, centralized system of control, which became prevalent in the Lake Victoria region of Kenya. Built as a fortified village, Thimlich Ohinga served defensive, economic, religious, and social functions. Archaeological research has discovered much about the urban structure and manufacturing of goods conducted within the community. As a former urban hub, many surrounding communities claim to have a connection to the history of Thimlich Ohinga, thus amplifying its local cultural importance.

By 1730 the Jok families began to colonise the South Nyanza Gulf and it is in this conquest where the Jo-Uyoma warriors had a role as skilled gladiators.

During their stay in Kanyamwa, Jo-Uyoma faced several challenges. The Kanyamwa and Kochia people used the Uyoma warriors to help them fight their battles. The Uyoma warriors acquired weapons and also learnt the art of making shields from Buffalo skins. They had shields made from buffalo skin that a spear cannot penetrate. They had large heavy spears known as *Tong Abaja*. This spear is so strong that it can tear the skin of a hipopotomus. The Uyoma warriors played their roles in the battle fields and won many battles, but incidentally they were never paid their mercenary dues as they expected. The Uyoma people demanded payment for services renderd as was the case in all battles in those days. In normal circumstances the warriors were usually paid in terms of a percentage of livestock raided. The warriors were usually given six cows and some shoats *Sheep and goats*. Jo-Uyoma started being disgruntled and this led to conflict among the three groups. The Kanyamwa and their neghbours were also getting uncomfortable with the high rate of population growth of Jo-Uyoma. It was also noted that the Uyoma people were unnecessarily arrogant due to their fighting skills and might which was clearly demonstrated during all the battles. Their wealth had grown beyond the kanyamwa and neighbours, due to cattle raiding. During their battles they raided livestock, property plus women and children. The capturing of women increased their population triple fold. The population and the wealth made the Chwanya off-springs uncomfortable and feared evident dominance of migrant Omia Ramul off-springs.

Due to inadequate assimilation in Kanyamwa, they were compelled to move back to ancestral land after a period of less than one generation. They were in Kanyamwa from 1790 to 1860s A.D.

THE PLANNED RETURN TO THE ANCESTRAL LAND

Before they moved back to the present Uyoma, one of the preparations was that they visited a woman magician; this magician advised them to develop a magical concotion with ingredients infused with human excreta, a rums offel *wen*. This magician's concotion was stirred in a guard. The magician's medicine was then given to Uyoma remnant lad/boy who was given the assignment of spilling the medicine in all the water points. The assignment was surpervised by Onuko jakanyojero *Jakabudha*. to ensure the boy carried the assignment as stipulated. *He collected alot of spy data especially during his drinking sprees.* Part of the concotion was put in the horn of the rum and pitched in the midst of Uyoma. After these libations the Uyoma old men went around Uyoma ululating the following "*Gima wachamoni be uchame*". This concotion that we are eating are you also eating it?

The Sakwa people kept on asking themselves "*Ango' ma Jo-Uyoma chamo ma wan to ok wa cham*" What is this concotion that the Uyoma people are eating and we are not eating. In the process the Sakwa people realized that there was something that was spilled in the water which they thought was palatable, and so they drunk more water from the water points. The excessive water in-take started to weaken the Sakwa people; this was the first strategy that was used for moving back to Uyoma. The purpose of this medicine is that it would weaken the Sakwa people and their livestock.

The second strategy was to consult the great magician *Jabilo* from Kanyamwa known as Ogalo wuon Tieng'o.Gor football club is named after the name of the son of this magician *This is the father of Gor Ogalo Named after the football club Gor Mahia*. Ogalo made various consultations with the forefathers of Jo-Uyoma and the spirits who drove him to give Jo-Uyoma the second strategy to return to promised motherland and settle peacefully and forever. The Uyoma representatives who consulted Ogalo were the following elders; Oguta wauga and Onyango wuon Otonde. Ogalo asked the Uyoma elders to bring with them different items in order of their family/clan seniority *duong' mar nyuol - chogo*.

The items were as follows: from Abiero wuod Menya Jokaodhiriany *Jokajore* a bull *Ruath Rapenda*, from Nyawanda Joka-Abudha one black hen with seven eggs *Si marateng kod tong' abiriyo*, from Oguta wauga Joka-Atweng'a a castrated bull *Ruath Buoch*, Jokokwiri a pregnant woman *Dhako mayach* Atieno Nyar Pambo, but also the wife of *Chi* Opedhi.Onuko from Kabudha a great spy travelled across the lake to Uyoma with the black hen with seven eggs incognito. He went and gave the hen and the seven eggs to Ahono Nyar Mbeda and she is the one who took the hen and the eggs to the slopes of *Got Naya*.The significance of this ritual was that if all the eggs were successfully hatched then Jo-Uyoma would The seven eggs represented the seven clans livinginUyoma. travel safely and settle peacefully in the promised ancestral land. Apparentlly the black hen hatched the seven eggs successfully as predicted by sooth sayer and magician *Janyakalondo*.

After this eventfull moment, feedback was sent to Ogalo and hence to the people of Uyoma.

Geke was assigned to take the siring bull *Ruadh Mapocho* from Jokajore across the lake in his boat to Uyoma. The purpose of the bull *Ruadhni was* to sire as many calves as possible, in the process the milk from the cows when consumed by the Sakwa men, would weaken them further. The milk was supposed to enhance the weakening process of the Sakwa people in addition to the water taken from the waterpoints that were already poisoned by the original concoction from the guards - *puga*. These two magics would weaken the Sakwa people to the extent that they would not resist the Uyoma attack or invasion.

According to Ogalo the magician, it was instructed that the day that Atieno delivers the Uyoma people shall move to their ancestral land carrying the placenta in a Luo knitted basket *adita*. The journey entailed crossing the Nyanza Gulf by boat because the gulf was now filled with water. The boat carried Atieno with her son, her husband Opedhi, the castrated bull, Nyagwara the owner of the boat and other relatives. The placenta was well packed in the basket and placed infrontal cabin of the boat. On arrival the placenta was buried at the peak of Got Naya. Opedhi settled with his family which included his three wives and the fourth wife Atieno, her son and the other senior children. This was the first arrivals of Uyoma people from Kanyamwa. The magician prophesised that the son of Atieno, Ogutu Anyieche would not die a natural death, like sickness or old age. He would die but in a battle field in defence of *Jo-Uyoma* and their ancestral land.this came to pass during the Mumbo Massacre of December 27th 1899

The Opedhi family and the remnant of Uyoma people that remained behind during the migration to Kanyamwa started sending signals to the Sakwa people that they should demarcate the boundaries properly because the owners of the promised land were soon coming back *Jo-Uyoma manodong nochako wacho ne josakwa mondo opidh kiewo maber weg lope biro*(miLuongo ni nyikwa weglowo)

The migration of Jo-Uyoma took the direction of Kendu Bay to Chula Rabuor *Ndere Island*; they took fleets of more than fifty boat trips. They landed at Kitari in Seme. The Seme people welcomed their kin with joy, Nyikal the grandfather of seme people was the cousin of Omia Ramul the grandfather of Jo - Uyoma. It is noted that during the journey Okoth Ongaro *Jakagwa* played a significant role. Okoth Ongaro was extremely tall slender athletic man, he navigated the depth of the lake using a stick and when he confirmed the children and young mothers could not drown is when he let them cross or ~~passes~~ pass through the water while the boats sailed back to collect the others.

This drawing is depicting Okoth Ongaro leading the crossing of shallow waters of Lake Victoria from the present Kendu bay to Seme

The Uyoma people temporarily settled among Jokadinga in Seme for almost one year in preparation of their movement to Thurmony this was in 1869 A.D. The preparation entailed spying, surveying and monitoring the activities of the Sakwa people. The Uyoma warriors were well armed with modern lethal weapons. Based on their military experience and improved weapons made in Kanyamwa and some imported from or captured from the hostile Southern Tanzanian Bantus.

They planned for almost one year to invade and overrun the Sakwa people to enter the Promised Land. The invasion of the Sakwa people started off tactfully with a first movement to Atsango (*Chuodho Kojuang*) in Asembo by the Uyoma warriors. To their utter amazement they found that the Sakwa people had built a fifteen to twenty kilometer fence with thorns all the way from Kadedi Beach at Rarieda to Kamariga Beach in Kagwa, Uyoma. The fence covered the narrow entry into Uyoma which is surrounded by the lake. This made their attack very difficult and they had to go back to the drawing board for a successful invasion of the Sakwa people. Jo-Uyoma knew very clearly that the Sakwa warriors were fierce in the tradional war fare and innovative approach was required for them to regain the land of their forefathers. Sakwa were well prepared for any Uyoma intrusion, and they knew that the Uyoma people were ruthless and mercyless.

PRAYERS BEFORE THE ONSLAUGHT

Oh Lord God

Obongo Nyakalaga

Who liveth amongst us but in the hidden

Modak apanda

Oh Lord God

Obongo Nyakalaga

The father of our forefathers

Nyasach Kwerewa

Oh Ramogi Ajwang our great grandfather

Nyasach kwarwa Ramogi Ajuang'

You begot Omia Ramul who begot the great Owila

Ni imiyowa Omia Ramul ma kwarwa Owila

Oh God and our Forefathers

Nyasach Kwerewa

Look yeh upon us during this time of war

Miwa jing'o gi teko e lweny ni

You all promised that we will over run our enemies when we come before you with these offerings and libetions

Oh God and our Forefathers we seek forgiveness of all our trespasses

Obong'o Nyakalaga kod Kwere wa yie uru kawuono uwenwa richo wa gi ketho wa

We beg thee for forgiveness

Wenwa richo wa wan jo ketho

Oh God and our Forefathers give us strength to overcome our enemies that today walking, trodding, grazing and tilling our ancestral land

Obong'o Nyakalaga gi Kwere wa miwa teko kod mijing'o mondo walo wasikwa modak, wuotho, kwayo jambgi kendo puro lope wa mane umiyo wa

Oh God and our Forefathers accept our prayers and offerings and bestow upon us and our warriors' health and strength.

Wabiro iru mondo uyie ukau chiwo kendo uwinj lambwa

Let the spears stay in the hands of our sons and scatter our enemies

Oh Obong'o Nyakalaga–yieuru kwayo wa umiwa mijingo' kod teko mondo tonge wa osiki e lwet jolwenywa kendo umi wasikwa oke.

Thanks be to God

Walami gi mago Obong'o

The new strategy to attack and overrun Sakwa was a guerilla war fare approach. One group of the warriors assembled at Aora Chuodho Kojuang' *Atsango*. Prayers and blessings were held at Rarieda led by Oginga Agidhi *Ruodh Uyoma,* Onyango Wuon Otonde and Osike Kirina *Jabilo* after which the four warrior groups were dispatched to their various positions.

The invasion started by burning the fence by the two warrior groups. Two groups would physically attack the Sakwa people from Mumbo and the other from Ruma. This attack was nick named the sandwich approach. In Luo this is known as *lwenj dino gi geng'o.,* in the modern term it would be said that' *wang'ni wadino nu.* The fence built by Jo-sakwa was very high; this meant that the traditional warfare of typical weapons and confrontation could not suffice on their own. The warfare entailed an attack on the fence and home with tactfull night operation. They lined up themselves along the great fence; this invasion was led by Yongo Awang' Mach and Onyango wuon Otonde. The two leaders were stationed all along the fence with their warriors at ten in the night that is Yongo Awang' Mach. The third and largest group of warriors was led by Onyango Wuon Otonde and was stationed in a position headed for Ruma for direct attack with normal war weapons, which included swords, matchets, spears and shields. Geke who had arrived in Uyoma earlier had prepared the Uyoma remnants and those he had travelled with for full-fledged war fare. Geke was the leader of the fourth and interial group which was stationed at Mumbo infront of the present Lieta Primary School.

It was agreed that Yongo would be stationed between the present Oyuga Aloo's home and Masala Primary School. It was agreed that Yongo would start burning the fence at midnight to alert the three other warrior groups to start the invasion and attack from their various positions. Yongo though a great warrior, he was a very impatient man and he kept on asking his colleagues, 'Do I start the fire now, I start the fire?' "*Awang'mach, awang' mach*?" hence the legendary name Yongo Awang' Mach. His colleagues knew his usual impatient character which was now very useful and they kept on telling him, "Yongo light the fire" "*Yongo wang mach*". They now formed a loud chorus *Yongo wang'mach, Yongo wang mach'.* The shouting and signal alerted their other groups and fire started gutting the fifteen kilometer fence and it was all over on any hill, bush and then into Sakwa homes. This caused panic and despondency among the Sakwa people who were awakened by the shouting burning fire everywhere. The Sakwa people started alerting their neighbors by cries and ululations that "Uyoma people have come and they are burning homes and looting our grain and properties wake up and run". *Yawa jouyma gi osechopo kendo wango' mier kendo gibiro mayo wa cham gi mwandu wa, chiew uru uringi, jogo osechopo.* Interestingly a woman from Ong'ala's home woke up and started fire on her granaries saying,

"I cannot leave food for the hungry Uyoma people. *Okanyal weyo chiemba ne joUyoma makech kayo mondo ocham, ber mondo awang'gi.* She actually burnt her granaries and the other granaries and the fire gutted the whole home and the neighbourhood. Her action was a blessing in disguise to Jo-Uyoma because Ong'ala was the highly respected man and also the leader of the Sakwa people.

People started panicking in the middle of the night, saying "If they have attacked and burned the leaders home, then who are we?" *Ka dala Ong'ala jatelo ema ose wang,' koro wan to wan nga' gini?*

With the intense and abrupt night attack the Sakwa people started running in panic towards Got Abiero and into their present settlement location.

By the wee hours of the morning all Sakwa people, except those who succumbed to surrender had left the Uyoma promised land by the Fore fathers namely Owila and Dilang'.

The map below shows the extent of the fence which at that time was massive project and it is estimated that it took Sakwa one year to erect this thorn fence. The thorn fence was as high as six foot resembling the current Maasai homesteads covered with thorns.

The Sakwa remnants or collaborators included the families of Onyango Ranger who begot Dr. OdundoAmbitho. They had and have maritrimonial relationship with Joka Owila. Onyango Ranger married Ligawafrom Kobar a Kawuor of Katwenga. Oluga the biological grand farther of John Mark Otito, married Ochieng the daughter of Ongala. Ongala was the leader of or ruoth Sakwa of Uyoma. He is the great Grandfather of Dr. Hon William Odongo Omamo.

The day following the night attack and invasion the Uyoma Elders led their warriors to Thurmony. The ceremony entailed the following; the warriors were led t to the Owila's grave stone, to sharpen their war spears on the stone signifying victory and confirming to Owila that they had lived to their promise as he had instructed at got Ng'iya.

Atieno gave birth to the promised son named Ogutu Anyieche on the fatal night of the Jo-Uyoma invasion on the Sakwa people.

The castrated bull was donated by Oguta Wauga that accompanied Atieno wife of Opedhi was then used as a sacrifice and it was slaughtered at Thurmony after the arrival of Jo-Uyoma warriors. The Uyoma elders led the warriors to feast on the bull ne *gi chuto ojuri.*

After the ceremony the looted grains, livestock and other properties were distributed to the grandmothers representing the families.

It is important to note that the grains that were looted from the Sakwa people helped Jo-Uyoma who had not ploughed or harvested for almost one year, during the great famine known as *Ke Ang'ieng laki 1871.* The famine was so severe that people ate the animal skins used as their bedding*s*

BAD BLOOD AND SIBLING WRANGLES

The Luos say that *Dar e kwe dak* this means that if relatives especially brothers, when they live far from each other the distance creates harmony and peace This may be true but in the case of Omia Ramul (Uyoma) and Wango (Kawango) it has taken over 100 years for this saying to apply (*Living separately creates family harmony*). All the same or on the other hand this saying is the origin of boys moving from their parental homes when they come of age, a man comes of age when his sons are teenagers and that the sons and daughters should never get married when they are still living at their grand fathers home stead *simba*.

Omia Ramul and Wango are the sons of Ramogi Ajwang' from the same mother, these two brothers grew up while supporting each other during their childhood at Got Ramogi. They separated when Omia Ramul moved to Uyoma (Thurmony) from Got Ramogi while Wango moved to the present Kawango or Mumias near River Wuoroya. When Omia and his offsprings lived in the present Uyoma, they were faced with famine; drought and hostile neighbours and they decided to seek refuge at their kin in Kawango. When Omia Ramul's offsprings moved to Kawango they went to live with their next of kin. Little did they know that living together would create a generational enemy that resulted into the worst enemies exhibiting the sibling wrangles spanning many many generations and culminating into Mumbo massacre engineered by the offsprings of Wango against their kin Omia Ramul?

It all started with Omolo Ng'ong'o (Baluhya pronounciation) or Omolo Ng'ongo during their stay in Kawango and youth fights that resulted into the death of Kawango youth. Omolo Ng'ong'o had used his roughness and uncouth games to drown the Kawango youths in to River Wuo Roya. The result did not go well with the Kawango family who demanded for a meeting to resolve the issue and an apology. Both meeting and apology did not take place, instead the Owila family (Jo-Uyoma) opted to go back to their ancestral land Thurmony today known as Uyoma from the word Oyuma and a corrupted pronounciation by the Baluhya as abayuma which means ja- Oyuma.

This separation caused ultimate bitterness, that Jo-Kawango pursued their kinsmen at Alego Kobare after their departure from Gunda Uyoma. Jo- Kawango wanted to revenge the death of their youths who were killed by Omolo Ng'ong'o. The Kawango teamed with Jo-Alego and Jo-Ugenya to attack Jo-Uyoma because Jo-Uyoma caused havock wherever they passed. On their way they had eloped with a girl from Alego, this girl is known as Atweng'a. They also raided Matar's home; Matar is the great grand father of Jo-Sakwa and an offspring of Ramogi Ajwang', incidentally he is also Owila's relative. Jo-Uyoma were saved from a massive attack from Alego and kawango by Le the brother of Amolo the second wife of Owila, he diverted them by directing them towards Yimbo and yet Jo-Uyoma were headed towards Asembo and temporarily settled in Abom.

It is unfortunate that the arrogance and the thurgish behavior of Jo-Uyoma defamed them in the whole region starting from Kawango, Alego, Abom, Uyoma, and Kanyamwa back to Uyoma with Jo-Sakwa and worse in the area of present Uyoma. The only relatives who were not hostile were Jo-Seme but specifically the Rado and Nyikal clans who are their kinsmen. These turmoils turned them into warriors and they had to learn to fight, their men were trained to be warriors from childhood.

Jo-Kawango, Gem, Ugenya hated Jo-Uyoma and for very good reasons. Uyoma became unpopular to the Kabaka Kingdom, Arab Slave traders, Muslims, the Christians and even to new arrivals, the British

Colonialists. Jo-Kawango developed relationships with all neigbours and visitors. They formed teams to raid Jo-Uyoma to get slaves and any other property they would find. Jo-Kawango benefited and became the regional leaders; the Kawango kingdom had influence in the present Nyanza and Western Provinces bordering the Kabaka on the Ugandan side, the Pokot, Nandi, Kisii and the Maasai areas which by then were all part of Eastern Uganda. The Kawango and Jo-Gem introduced modern education system borrowing from the Kabakas through the British. The Missionaries introduced Christianity, the Muslims introduced Islam and the religions flourished in the region leaving out Uyoma. In Gem Odera Ulalo and Odera Akang'o promoted education and Christianity in Gem and it spread to Alego. The evidence is old religious centers such as Maseno, Yala in Luo land. Jo-Kawango embraced Islamic religion and today they have leading population in Western Kenya and only second to the Coastal region in regard to Muslim population. Jo-Uyoma completely rejected Islam because it was associated with slave trade through Kawango and the Kabaka, they also rejected Christianity because it was associated with the Mumbo massacre.

Even though Christianity found its footings after World War II in Uyoma, very few embraced Christianity until the late 1950s and beyond, this was the same with education. The only Christian and education center was at Chianda.

Uyoma was endowed with wealth ranging from fertile and productive land, very high population of livestock and plenty of fish. Because it is in the interior of Luo land, it had very few visitors; they were hostile to strangers based on their historical experiences.

Uyoma was built on warriorship and this has influenced many men and women from Uyoma to exhibit this character even in the modern society.

This behavior of suspicion has been positive and negative to Jo-Uyoma, historically Jo-Uyoma had bad experience with their neighbours right from the time they came from Got Ramogi the same hostility was exhibited in Kawango, in kanyamwa they were misused as war merceneries, they rebelled and returned to their ancestral land in Uyoma only to be faced with hostile Sakwa. The Kawango organized deliberate revenge of long term sibling enemity. The slave traders intruded Uyoma via the lake from the Kabaka kingdom.The British forcefully recruited Uyoma youth into the World Wars I and II, Jo-Uyoma never knew the origins and objectives of these wars. The British forced Jo-Uyoma to contribute livestock, food and other resources to the construction of the *lunatic* railway line.This suspicion is still alive in Uyoma that even todate a stranger enters Uyoma they are constantly interrogated as in who they are and where they are going. This has promoted security in the area and reduced theft, thuggery and cattle rustling

THE FINAL SETTLEMENT IN UYOMA

After all the events at Thurmony the Jo-Uyoma were dispatched to various parts of Uyoma in the following manner by the Elders led by their leader Ruoth Oginga Agidhi:

1. The Kobong' people went and settled at Nyawita, Pala, Kobong' and Gwena in Rachar Sub-Location
2. The Kabudha (Jokojal) moved to two different sites namely
    2.1 The Northern side known as Kabudha ma Gem Oranga, they settled at Kakremba, Matara, Ombonya and Rageng'ni. They today occupy Ochienga' and Rageng'ni Sub-Locations.
    2.2 The other family group of Kabudha occupied; Rabel, Ndigwa and Lwala, they are as today known as Kabudha ma Naya, they occupy the Southern part of Uyoma.

    2.3 The Kogweno family occupied part of Naya area but moved later back to Karachuonyo in Kogweno the present Homabay County.

3. The Wamiembe family never moved, they remained at Madundu
4. The Kalir and Kanyikela settled at Nyangoye.
5. The Katwenga' group moved to Lela, Kasiri, Got kotieno *today Got Kachola*, Wayaga, Malanga, Rabuor, Migowa and Okela.
6. The Kabuong' remained at Mumbo the present Lieta Sub-Location.
7. The Kanyigoro people moved to Ndere, Nyakongo and Manyuanda.
8. The Kobunga people moved to Misori Kaywaya and between Ndere and Lwala.
9. The Kale *Asembo* people moved to Rombo Moti, Kayundi, Ukunja, Ralak and Ndiru. *After their removal later only remnants were left*. Today this area is occupied by Kotieno/Kakoth, Kajore and Jo-Kisumu.
10. The Kagwa people had two groups, the main group remained all along at Ngero *Kagwa Primary and Secondary Schools* area, the other group settled at Nyamasore and Rageng'ni.
11. The Kokwiri people remained in Atsango or Nyang'oma and occupied the area of Ougo *Kalandin*, Mabinju, Ong'ielo and Miyare. That was the area of Kokwiri called Ywaya. There were Sori in Omia hence the place was nicknamed Sori Ka Ywaya. The Ko-Kwiri people later joined their siblings in Uyoma and today they occupy the Western part of Uyoma known as Uyoma Kokwiri.
12. . The Wagoro and the Kobunga people never moved and remained at Tanga, Wambisa and the current Wagoro area.
13. The Sigulu people joined the Wamiembe at Madundu and now live in Naya Sub-Location

Jo-Uyoma settled after the invasion as explained above, but many issues cropped up among the inhabitants. The clan and sibling wrangles resulted into some changes in the final settlement which prevails up todate.

The settlement took the typical Luo traditional building infrastructure format which entailed the following; in normal circumstances the first wife's house is built with the door directly facing the main gate, she is known as *mikayi*. The second wife's house is built on the right hand side of the first wife's house, she is known as *Nyachira,* her door faces the gate halfway or sideway. The third wife's house is built on the left hand side of the first wife's house, she is known as *Reru,* her door also faces the main gate halfway or sideway. The fouth was *Diwinja* The order goes on in that pattern for all future wives, ie fourth, fifth, sixth and so and so on. The order of the Jo-Uyoma settlement took this traditional order into consideration. Owila's first wife is Ngo', his second is Amolo, the third wife is Adeka and the fourth wife is Gori.

Ngo's offsprings Jo-Komolo Ngo'ngo and Jo-Kokelo settled at the present Kobong' and Rachar of Central Uyoma. Amolo was the second wife and her offsprings are Jo-Kojal the first son (Kabudha) and Onege the second son (Katweng'a) moved to the right hand side of Ngo' which is Naya and this area is on the Eastern side of the first house. Adeka is the third wife and her offsprings are joka- Liech, Jo-Kowuor and Jo-Kokwiri, they moved to the Western side or the left hand side of Ngo' the first wife. Gori the fourth wife is also the sister of Ngo' the first wife. Her offspring is Jo-Kotwal moved next to his maternal cousin (brother) in Central Uyoma.

MARKING THE BOUNDARY WITH SAKWA

The Kagwa people were known as great warriors and with strong magicians, their fame for these two aspects were known by all their neighbors especially Jo-Sakwa and the Jo-Uyoma in general. The Sakwa people also had very strong warriors and the two neighbors were always careful not to provoke each other. Kagwa people were also known for their cattle or livestock raiding. It should be noted that during the people's movements the Sakwa people originally moved from Kawango to Alego then to other parts of Nyanza later they reunited to form the present Sakwa Community mainly found in Bondo Sub-County. They are the great grandchildren of Matar the son of Wango.

A meeting of Sakwa and Uyoma elders was held at the present Masala area in the presence of warriors from both sides. The elders disagreed and started abusing each other. The warriors according to Luo tradition are not allowed to respond or even make positive or negative gestures. The Sakwa people insisted that their boundary with Uyoma should be at Masala (*Nyarwenya*) where they held the meeting, but Jo-Uyoma insisted that the Sakwa suggestion was not right and they insisted on Got Abiero and Kipasi as the boundary. The meeting was so heated that they started asking their sons. "If this is how the Sakwa are behaving then we must teach them a lesson". The Sakwa people responded by asking, "When did the Uyoma weaklings and cowards ever face the great Sakwa men or did you assume we will bring our wives to the battlefield". Another Jasakwa elder said "This time we do not need warriors or old men but just our young girls. The Uyoma Elders retorted and told the Sakwa that we are only giving you this evening to move, if you do not move by tomorrow evening then we will capture your girls and turn them to wives without dowry, we will raid you and capture your young wives and only grandmothers will be left. We will destroy these weaklings we see behind you. The meeting abruptly ended with Sakwa summarizing, "You talk of tomorrow, any day you touch anything that belongs to Sakwa, you Kagwa will all be dead before we rise upon the rest of Uyoma as we have done before.

After this meeting all the Sakwa people went back to get ready for battle. In Uyoma all those Kagwa relatives selected their best warriors in readiness to attack and destroy Sakwa community.

Jo-Uyoma spared their best warriors including Onoka Maugo, Omondo Oguta, Odundo Openda, Nange Oluga, Ongoro Nyapende (Known for being a very handsome man), among others.

The Uyoma did not want Onoka to join the lead warriors, but he insisted that the Sakwa could not insult his elders, it was better he died than witness that kind of insult.

The Uyoma knew well that the Sakwa warriors were very strong but this time they assured the elders that they would call Sakwa to battle face to face. The day after the meeting the Uyoma warriors dared the Sakwa warriors to reach Masala and face the wrath. The brave Sakwa warriors sent obvious signals that they were going to stamp their authority in Masala. Before they reached the point of the last meeting in Masala, the Uyoma warriors moved forward and the battle raged for more than four hours. At the fifth hour the Uyoma warriors started to slowly overpowering their opponents. By mid-day the Sakwa moved backwards and Uyoma warriors pursued them and by 2.00 pm the Sakwa warriors were getting tired and yet the Uyoma main warriors were now joining the battle starting with Nange Oluga and Ongoro Nyapende. Then the rest of lead warriors joined battle for the final assault. Onoka Maugo moved forward to lead the final assault; they bashed Sakwa warriors senselessly until they reached near Got Abiero. When they reached present Thim Primary School, Onoka remained behind the enemy line at the river next to Kipasi junction. He moved to face the remnant warriors and unfortunately he was caught up in the thorny bushes of arcacia tree and *okwato* and could not fight. Three Sakwa warriors went close to him and dared him, before they could kill him with their spears, he shouted "Your spears are not strong enough and stinging like a tsetse fly take a real man's spear and kill me" *Tonge u go tindo,kaw uru tonga mar dichwo mondo unega-go, un joma tongegi ok nyal kata nego suna.un joma nyap gi negauru gi tonga to ka ekama tong' mar Uyoma gi Sakwa nobedie!!!* One of the Sakwa warriors moved into the bush where Onoka was stuck took his spear and Onoka shouted at him "You weakling kill me with my spear so that the boundary is settled. They killed Onoka Maugo in cold blood and batte ended and the boundary was demarked until today. History has it that the Sakwa warriors and whole of Uyoma and neighborhood could not believe that a man can be so brave to the extent that he asks his enemies to kill him with his own spear and to die clenching his teeth and hands signifying bravery and victory.

The thorny bushes where Onoka was killed along river ahedo exists to date

As a symbol of victory or defeat they tore Onoka's body into pieces and took the pieces as war souvenir.

The Kagwa people were used as a buffer to cushion the Uyoma from Sakwa.The Kanyigoro of Asembo were also very hostile to the Sakwa expansionist

Boundary song

Omondo majaUyoma nodhure kuot x2

Adhuro majaUyoma nodhuro ekuot x2

Nyithindo waparo ndalo

Ja- Uyoma

Even after the so called boundery demarcation with Sakwa todate it is not definitive. The shield and Onoka's death spot was the assumed boundery between Uyoma and Sakwa.

THE RELATIONSHIP BETWEEN UYOMA AND ASEMBO

We cannot dicuss the Kale remnants in Uyoma before articulating their roots and relationship with Owila and the Jo-Uyoma.

Asembo has double relationship with Jo-Uyoma; one relationship is maternal while the other is paternal. Let us start with the maternal relationship.

THE MATERNAL RELATIONSHIP WITH ASEMBO

The Kale offsprings are great grandchildren of Ramogi Ajuang (II). We can trace the Kale and Jo-Uyoma maternal relationship from Silwal who was the great grand child of Ramogi Ajuang (II). The family lineage goes as follows; Ramogi is the father of Nyanduogi, Nyanduogi is the father of Oriambwa, Oriambwa is the father of Ujal, Ujal is the father of Kini, Kini is the father of Silwal, Sabong' and Okidi. Silwal is the father of Le and Amolo. Amolo the daughter of Silwal was married to Owila as second wife *dhako mar ariyo*, she is the grandmother of the Joka-Abudha and Joka-Atwenga' in Uyoma. Le is the father of Nyakala *Joka-Nyakala*, Abondo *Joka-Abondo* Kia *Joka-Kia*, Oduong' *Assimilated in Kaabondo*. Adeka the daughter of Le was the third wife of Owila and her offsprings are the Kokwiri clan in Uyoma and Karateng' in Kisumu County *Jo-kisumu Karateng'*.

THE PATERNAL RELATIONSHIP WITH ASEMBO

The paternal relationship can be traced from Omia Ramul whose offsprings are Dilang' and Owila. Both Dilang' and Owila are paternal and maternal brothers from Odhiriany and Otimbla *Nya Kobunga*. They both migrated to Kawango and lived harmoniously together. During their exodus to Uyoma they shortly lived in Alego kobare in a place presently known as *Gunda Owila* or Gunda Uyoma. Dilang' had two wives, the first wife begot Ajore only, the second wife begot Okise and Owuor. The first wife always pittied herself as barren because she had only one child known as Ajore, In Luo a barren woman is known as *Lur*. In her constant pitty party reference people also refered to her as Madam Baren, in Luo she was refered to as *Lu r-ni*. This constant negative reference and despise brought bad blood between the Co-wives and their offsprings. Dilang and preferred second wife plus his aging mother Otimbla unceremoniously moved from their temporary home in Alego through Gem Akala towards the Eastern part of Asembo at Kokise. Part of Dilang's offsprings moved to present Asembo. The Dilang's second wife offsprings, the Kowuor and the Kokise that moved to Asembo are settled at Omia Malo, Omia Diere and Omia Mwalo, they are today found in East Asembo of Rarieda Sub-County. Their ailing and aging Grandmother, Otimbla died and was buried at the present site Kokise Polytechnic.

The Dilang's first wife's offsprings are known as Jo-Kadilur that went to Uyoma with Owila Offsprings are today settled in Ochieng'a and Masala Sub-Locations and are also known as Jo-Kajore Ajore had two sons, Tinda and Ochieng' Opuk Laro. It is worth noting that Ajore is the father of Tinda who carried Owila's Gravestone to Madiany. While Ochieng' Opuk Laro inherited Owila's third wife and begot Okwiri, the patriarch of Ko-Kwiri Clan of West Uyoma.

All through history whenever Jokabudha and Katwenga' had any battle, Jo-Kajore who are their first cousins would always support them. Technically these families should not intermarry. The Jokajore are not related by blood to Jo-Kale *Asembo*.

SEMBO ASEMBO

Jo- Kale people were usually very arrogant and war- like and they always despised Jo-Uyoma especially at social forums like courting of brides, drinking ceremonies and or funerals. In one such occasion Opiyo Kwach from Kale stoned (*Golero*) Ongoro Nyawende. Kwenya Wuod Alindi was also despised by these kale people. Ojal the daughter Agutu from Kale was eloped by Ouya Kanyawanga as the normal tradition in those days. That very night Ojal lamented and abused the Uyoma people, 'You black ugly men with rotten teeth cannot match or even marry beautiful, brown soft girls from Kale, therefore tomorrow you will face the wrath of my brothers. *Ojal nyar Agutu jakale noywak matek ka wacho ni Un Jo-Uyoma ma rotenge marorichni ma leke gi otop gi, ok nyal kendo nyar kalando ma jaber kama, kiny unuwuor yawuotwa gi owetena.*

Incidentally the next day Ojal's brothers, Omogo, Omach Rachore and other kale men attended a courting ceremony of Othina the daughter of Kabudha, they were told of an incident that involved their sister Ojal who was forcefully eloped by Ouya Ka Nyawanga.

The next day the Kale people mobilized their young men to attack the Uyoma people to rescue their sister, as they moved; they found their enemies waiting for them and hell broke loose. The fighting started in very high tone and many injuries were recorded but the worst was the breaking almost to amputation of Otieno Amire's leg. The following day Owenda Akoth killed Nyanya ja Kochieng'. During the appeasing of the spirits *Tero buru* of Nyanya Ja Kochieng', at this ceremony Ojuka (Grandfather of Johny ojuka of Naya) killed Apiyo wuod Otweyo.

These various incidences amounted to great hostility between the Kale and Kamkong' (Kajore and Kabudha). At this juncture Kamkong' insisted that Kale must move out of Uyoma. The Uyoma people consulted their magician (*jabilo*) known as Andhonga, to find ways of moving kale from Uyoma. He instructed them to take an old goat so that the Kale people can feast on it. The second instruction was to kill rats and put them in the Kale's granaries. The third instructions were to capture a live antelope and dress it with a napkin (Tweyo ne mwanda chieno). The idea was to appease the newly married Ojal. Goye wuod Oduru was sent to carry out this assignment.

Now the die was cast and the battle *raged*, it was pitched at Masala. This battle went on overnight as stalemate, but in the morning the Kale people started retreating backwards. The Uyoma warriors overwhelmed them and started chasing them; they were chasing and escorting them up to Rarieda. The chasing and escorting in Luo is known as *sembo* hence the name Asembo as they are known to date. In this battle Obonyo Obor was killed by Onyango Gweno wuod Ogilo Jakabudha. The body of Obonyo Obor was sliced into pieces by Andhonga and was buried under the Egyptica tree *Otho* found at Rimu Matara the present Kunya next to the home of Oyaro Oneko. The Uyoma and Asembo boundary was fixed at Rarieda, the final battle field.

It was that day that Ochere and Yongo went to look for brides from Seme. On reaching Rarieda they were told that Nyanya Jaka Ochieng Owenda and Ja-Akoth were in fierce batle between Nyalunya and Ruma. The place was infested by warlings and they decided to follow different paths. They parted ways honorable for security reasons .Yongo decided to follow the reeds through Rageng'ni to Okela.Ochere went through Nyagoko if he went westwards through Nyagoko to Okela. Suprisingly enough both arrived at the same time hence the say *Nyasach Yongo ok en Nyasach Ochere* 'Yongo's god is Not

Ochere's god'. Yongo was a great magician and most of his offsprings such as Richard Monye Ochieng' wuon Okela, Yongo Alosa a.k.a Alosa KiromYongo *Just put it in writing not verbal*, Jack Otieno Owenda is the grandson of his granddaughter Regina nyar Okuku ka Yongo who was married in Sakw. a Okuku son of Yongo, Regina daughter of Okuku , regina mother ofAbonyo and Abonyo bore Jack Owenda.

THE UYOMA ASSIMILADOS

The Owila offsprings have lived alongside neighbours who are relatives or who have turned into relatives through marriage or association. These relatives therefore have been assimilated and form the greater Uyoma Household. Those who are assimilated are refered to as the Uyoma Assimilados giving them the rightful ownership of this ancesteral land of Omia Ramul the son of Ramogi and Owila the patriarch of Uyoma.

The reference of assimilado is used positively in this book, in the English Dictionary Assimilate means to absorb a group of people in to a community. After the assimilation they become part and parcel of the respective community. In this case the Uyoma assimilados are those people who have been absorbed in the Owila community and they are Jo-Uyoma by all rights.

Apart from the cultural and traditional assimilation, the legal framework gives assimilados legal ownership of the land where they have settled. Clear refrence can be made to civil case no. 188 of 1958 between Andronico Obara Ja-Uyoma and Enock Akowa Ja-Sakwa which was brought before Shadrack Malo, President of the Native Tribunal Court in Kisumu.

The complainant Mr.Andronico Obara lost the case on the ground that the people of Sakwa who left their land had lost the ownership but those who remained retained the ownership.

In this case Andronico Obara was claiming to be the original Ja-Uyoma known in Luo as *Nyakwar Wuon Loo or Nyikwa weg Lope.* While Enock Akowa was termed as a temporary settler known negatively in Luo as *Jadak* or even worse *Ja-Kowiny or Misumba.*

In the ancient Roman Empire all assimilados except the slaves were given the right to vote. The Biblical Saint Paul who graduated from the University of Rome was a Jew who became a fully fledged citizen of the Roman Empire.

In the Muslim World in Medinah Assimilados Madinah were given ownership or citizenship through the constitution of Madinah.The constitution of Madinah was the first written constitution dealing with a pluristic society. The constitution gave the world some new conceipts. This was intergrating all Muslims from different places, races, tribes, the immigrants and the local Muslims as one Ummah- the spiritual Ummah. Muhammed gave the concept that Muslims belonging to any race or place anywhere are one Ummah or one people or community.

Similar cases are found in Sierra Leone and Mozambique where assimilados have acquired citizenship and land ownership with full socio-cultural and legal recognition.

The Uyoma assimilados discussed here below are as follows: Jo-Asembo, Kabuong', Kagwa, Sakwa, Wagoro, Kobunga, Kalir, Wamiembe, Wahondo and the Kasiemba.

JO-ASEMBO

Once upon a time Jo-Asembo and Jo-Uyoma lived as siblings based on their relationships. The relationships were both maternal and paternal. In the process of removing Jo-Asembo from Uyoma, some of their kins were left behind in Uyoma. Some of the members of the following clans remained in Uyoma for various reasons;

Ko-Ochieng': The Ko-Ochieng' clan is found in around Ruma and Aram. Such families include Mzee Ibrahim Nyanya.

Ka-Nyikela: The Kanyikela clan is found mostly in Central Asembo but some of their kin are found in Masala and includes Mzee Manyala Ong'ombe's family.

Kakia: The Kakia clan is predominantly found in central Asembo but their kin are found in Masala and Ochieng'a Sub-locations in Uyoma. The family of Ismail Odola Okara, Auko Wuon Adita and Jo-Kobambo are among the Kakia families in Uyoma.

Ko-kidi: The Ko-Kidi clan is predominantly found in South West Asembo but their kinsmen in Uyoma are found in Ruma, Aram and Lusi in Masala Sub-Location. Okidi is the son of Silwal. He migrated to Kisumo long time ago. In 1908 Chief Otumba persuaded them to come back and settled them in Ruma within the administrative boundary of Uyoma. They form the families of Kale who are in Asembo. The early settlers of Kokidi were Jonathan Omia, Alaro, Muga, Odwar and others. They are now fully assimilated with the people of Uyoma

KABUONG' CLAN

The clan of Kabuong' is originally from Alego. Owila's son called Onege married Buong's daughter known as Atweng'a. While Jo-Kowila were on transit through Alego, they moved with Buong's family to the present Uyoma. Kabuong' currently settled in Lieta, West Katweng'a and Masala Sub-Locations. The family of Onege are called Jo-Katwenga' named after their Grand mother Atweng'a Nyar Buong'.

Professor Otumba Ouko of Maseno University comes from Kabuong' clan and lives next to Chianda High School in Katwenga' amongst his kinsmen.

The Katweng'a clan does not intermarry with the Katieno family of Kabuong' clan and by origin Kabudha clan was not allowed to marry the offsprings of Kabuong'.

KAGWA CLAN

The Kagwa community has her origins from the Baganda of Uganda, they migrated to the present Uyoma in 1856 due to sibling and clan wrangles during the reign of Kabaka Suna. The two clans of Kagwa community from the Baganda Kingdom are Gwala and Waganda. The Kamo is another clan in Kagwa but they are the descendants of Ramogi Olum the grandfather of Ramogi Ajuang'II. They lived among the Jagero and the Bamogera of Baganda. They first settled in Alego, Sakwa and finally came down to Uyoma while Jo-Uyoma were still living in Kawango. The Kagwa community fought alongside Jo-Uyoma in the battle against the Sakwa people, Jo-*Sakwa* and the Jo-Asembo *kale*.

The Kagwa clans rightfully occupy Kagwa Sub-location in West Uyoma, some of their siblings have spread to Ochienga' and Rageng'ni Sub-Locations of East Uyoma.

The great Oruko Makasembo who was the first Senator of Central Nyanza comes from Kagwa- the Waganda clan. The long serving politician and also magician Zakayo Abonyo Oyombe and Domnic Otiende Omenya comes from Omenya – the Kamo clan. The long serving freedom fighter and politician Edwin Onyango Radier comes from Kagwa among the Kagwala clan.

The mother of the doyen of opposition politics in Kenya, Jaramogi Oginga Odinga of Sakwa comes from Kagwa, he is also named after Chief Oginga Agidhi of Uyoma. It is interesting to note that these three Kagwa clans intermarry.

SAKWA

The Sakwa people are great grand children of Matar, who was the grandson of Wanga, the brother of Omia Ramul the grandfather of Uyoma Patriarch, Owila

During the battle of Uyoma with the Matar clan, the Matar clan would pitch battle within the bushes, reappear and disappear rattling the bushes and hence Jo-Uyoma developed the strategy of carefully listening to the rattles. These bush rattles are known in Luo as *Sakni* hence the name Jo-Sakwa.

Even though there were many battles of supremacy and ownership between Jo- Sakwa and Jo- Uyoma. Some families were left behind in Uyoma. These include the Onyango Rang'er's and Okayo Awuor families. Both of the above families have matrimonial relationship with Jo-Kosewe of Kunya. These two factors have given them substantial ownership and identity in Uyoma.

THE KALIR

The Kalir clan comes from the Langi community of Uganda, they came from a place called Lira, hence Kalir. Lira is the current Langi District Headquater of Uganda. Joka-Lir is found in West Uyoma and East Uyoma *Nyamasore and Ukunja* areas. Other Kalir siblings can be found in Rieny Kowuoyo in South Nyanza.

The former President of Uganda Dr. Milton Obote comes from Kalir of Langi tribe in Uganda. During the Obote regime, many people from Uyoma got employment opportunities in Uganda because of this connection, even his driver was from Uyoma. The saying goes that many Luos dissappered into the Ugandan banana plantations with *guangala*. When Obote was ousted, some of the Luos came back to Kenya. The majority remained in Uganda and became Uganda Luo assimilados.

Bishop Abanga' Owenda who is a lecturer at Technical University of Kenya comes from Kalir clan in Nyamasore.

THE WAGORO CLAN

Wagoro is a Sub-clan of the Amagoro clan of Teso. The Teso are Nilotes with similar origin with the Luos, they have similar relationship with the Kalenjin, Turkana and the Maasai communities.

The Wagoro settled in the present Uyoma towards the end of the 18th Century. They are found in West and East Uyoma.

The Wagoro are active in the Social, Political and Economic developments. The second Luo *Ker* Pastor Joel Omer was from Wagoro in Karachuonyo, he is also the father of the prominent politician Mama Pheobe Asiyo. The Uyoma second Colonial Chief Paul Moyi Okweso also hails from Wagoro, his grandson Dr. Joseph Okweso who contested the Rarieda Parliamentary seat in 2013 is from Wagoro.

THE KOBUNGA CLAN

The Kobunga people are of Nilotic origin from Sudan, they settled in Osindo in the present Uyoma in the mid 17th Century.

Initially they prevented Jo-Uyoma (*omias*) from reaching or accessing the water point at Osindo. The Luo word preventing or hindering is known as Osindo

Otimbla was the daughter of Kobunga. Otimbla was the wife of Odhiriany who bore Dilang' and Owila. Owila the patriarch of Uyoma hence the blood relationship. Jo-Kobunga are found in west Uyoma around Osindo.

THE WAMIEMBE

The Wamiembe came from Sigulu Island in Uganda and came to Kenya across Lake Victoria to the present Southern part of Uyoma *Naya* mid 18th Century.

Miembe and his Wife Nyamwai stayed in the present Nyamwai Island facing Luanda Kotieno near Kamin Oningo Beach. After the death of his wife Nyamwai, he moved to the dry land and found no inhabitant around that place.

Miembe had the following sons Kimaya, Misenya, the largest family today in Uyoma among the Miembe, Misuru some are found in Kanyamkago in South Nyanza, Madinda and Midimo some are in Kanyamkago, Kasigunga and Kakmie.

The Wamiembe were not Nilotes, they came speaking Bantu language with phrases such as ''*abalaitaje, abalaingombe* ………''

The wamiembe have been assimilated by the Luos and today speak pure dhoLuo.

The have some of the relatives in Kanyamkago *The Kago Ramoth*.

THE WAHONDO

The Wahondo community first occupied the area around Naya in South Uyoma before they migrated to live among the Suba community in Mbita District. Remnants of the Wahondo community were left behind in and they still live in Uyoma at Wahondo. Those living in Homa bay County also carried the same name of Wahondo. The late Senator Otieno Kajuang' comes from Wahondo clan.

THE KASIEMBA

They came from Sigulu Island through Lihanda to Uyoma Naya. They came around 1900 during the building of the East African Railway line. They were led by Ogutu Omoro Muberi who landed at Nyamanga Beach. From Sigulu. They lived among the Wawere of Rusinga Island and as they crossed to Uyoma some were left behind. On arrival in Uyoma, they were welcomed by Mirau Obingo who was their kin. They lived with the Mirau's for over ten years before establishing their own respective homes. The Mubei family includes Ogutu Omoro, Ousa Muberi and Ogola Muberi. The Kasiemba community are mainly fishermen and they run many businesses. They have developed Luanda Kotieno into a thrieving business centre. Luanda Kotieno is named after Otieno wuon Ousa and is the gateway to Mbita in Homa Bay County.

THE COMING OF THE WHITE MAN

The coming of the Whiteman was predicted by Mboga Wuon Otieno. He told Jo-Uyoma that some people will invade them. They have weapons resembling cooking spoon *oluth kuon* that spits fire and kills instantly. They will defeat Jo-Uyoma as they have done elsewhere and turn them into slaves. These people have light skin resembling pre-mature babies *Bogno*. Mboga was dismissed by Jo-Uyoma.

Before the coming of the whiteman the Uyoma boundaries were very clearly demarkated with Asembo driven up to Rarieda and Sakwa smoked up to Got Abiero and hence the other side of the boundary. With the boundary demarked Uyoma turned their attention to wealth creation, they started with livestock restocking program. They lobbied for livestock from their relatives mainly from Yimbo, Seme, Kanyamwa, Alego, Gem and even Kawango. With the black cotton soil and wide grazing land, the livestock grew and increased immensely. Jo- Uyoma then turned to group and clan farming; they made sure that every woman had a cereal granary as a policy; they ensured that policy was that that the adequate food stock could see them through season. Ten years after the boundary demarcation Uyoma grew to be the leading granary of the Luo land with abundant food, livestock and other prodduces.

It is at this time that the slave traders started coming to Uyoma, the main suspected agent was Mboga who lived at the Lake shore in Misori. He had built several fishing boats, it is these boats that he used to get livestock from Kanyamwa and Mbita and he became a wealthy man. When the slave traders first arrived in Uyoma from Uganda, they met Mboga and started slave trafficking. He made various business trips to the Buganda kingdom.

One documentary proof of the slave trade is the capturing of Muche Nyar Ajemo at Kunya Sori, never to be traced todate. Muche was the third wife of Osewe the fourth grandmother of the author of this book - Lwande Oneko.

Mboga is the one that told or predicted to the Uyoma people that a white human being resembling a premature born baby *nyabogno* would come to conquer Uyoma. He told the Uyoma people these people have very complicated weapons and one of them resembles the large spoon or stick for cooking ugali *Oluth kuon* .People laughed at Mboga's prediction as a *Mister know all and know nothing*. How could some strangers attack great Uyoma warriors whatever the weapon, their defeat of Sakwa, Asembo and the war excellence they exhibited in Kanyamwa and even the various battles they have fought. Who could shake Jo-Uyoma and with all this wealth (*ngat mane manyalo buogo Jo- Uyoma kata Obigi ang'o? Uyoma nigi thuondi mag lweny omiyo wan kod mwandu moromo ok waLuor!!!*).

And so it came to pass that Mboga wuon Otieno was right and History has the following:

In August 1884, Otto Von Bismark Chancellor of the Imperial Federation of Germany convened the Berlin conference in which Africa was to be partitioned by the Imperialists. Kenya and Uganda were placed under the British possession. Africans were not consulted. In August 1893 Kenya and Uganda were now under the British Protectorate, and towards the end of the 19th Century. The Kenya Uganda Railway had reached Lumbwa towards Kisumu. The British first conquered Uganda, Uyoma became part of Uganda, it was in the Eastern Province of Uganda. The Provincial Commissioner of Eastern Province of Uganda was Mr C.W Hobly *Obilo*. Some of the communities in Eastern Province of Uganda such as the Baganda, the Wango, the Gem, the Seme, the Sakwa and the Asembo had already agreed to work with the British. Jo-Uyoma were known for their hostility towards all neighbors based on their past history and experience. They were also very arrogant because of their wealth and war like behavior.

Every community had their leaders and warriors, the Baganda had Kabaka Mutesa, the Wango had Mumia Ashiundu, the Asembo had Adhola and Mien Olanda, the Gem had Odera Akang'o, Sakwa had Onyango Randar, Yimbo had Ogutu wuon Kipapi, Kanyamwa had Gor Kogalo, Ugenya had Lala ka Banda and Nyawade wuod Ojak, Kano had Lwanda Magere, Uyoma had Mboga wuon Otieno, Nganyi ja Umuri, Alego had Tawo Ogot and Ng'ong'a wuon Odima, Seme had Nyagudi wuod Ogambi, Kisumu had Ogola wuod Ayieke, Okore wuod Ogonda, Olang'o wuod Odido, Siala Kaduol / Uriri Gem had poka woud Okumu among others.

Even Uyoma had their leader known as Mboga wuod Otieno from Kokwiri whose public relations went beyond Uyoma to places like Mbita and Kanyamwa on the opposite side of the Lake. He was also friendly to all the other neighbors up to Kawango, and had made connections with other communities plus his long standing friendship with the Kabaka Mwanga of the Buganda. Eastern Province Headquarters was at Mumias. Mr.C.W Hobly gave instructions that all communities under his area of administration were to be taxed and give material support to the construction of the Uganda railway line including tailes of killed rats to the Provincial headquarters to demonstrate that they were helping in fighting against the plague outbreak. All other communities had complied except Uyoma.

Mr.C.W Hobly made a deliberate effort to incooperate the Uyoma people to collaborate and contribute food and other materials towards the construction of the Railway line. They sent a message to Jo-Uyoma for a formal meeting to address development issues of the Province. The Uyoma Elders and Opinion Leaders were under the Chairmanship of Mboga Wuon Otieno. Mboga was the proclaimed Uyoma leader appointed by the people. The following noted personalities attended this meeting. Aloo Oyuga the owner of this land, Anyiri Kosando grandfather of Dr. Nick Ogola of Maseno Univesity, Ongalo Mijuka, Osike Kirina *Jabilo*, Opao, OLuoch Abaki,Oluga Dipondo, Oyaro Dipondo Otieno Osogo *Jalweny*, Molo Nyadundo *Jalweny* and all other Uyoma leaders. Every clan of Uyoma was represented. The meeting was held at Othoch Nyamarimba, behind Rageng'ni Centre.

Mr.C.W Hobly group was led by Odera Ulalo from Gem as the Head of the Mission accompanied by administrative officers from Asembo, Seme, Sakwa and other collaborating communities leaders. The objective of this meeting was to seek the cooperation of Uyoma people with the British Government and in this instance there were urgent issues of collaboration to be addressed.

The issues to be addressed were as follows:

- Donating land for agri-business to the White people
- Paying regular tax to British Administration for development of Nairobi, where Uyoma people would get housing and employment. The tax would also cater for supply of clothes and beddings for the Uyoma people
- Supply of livestock to the people constructing the Railway line in Lumbwa
- Grinding and supply of flour mills to the railway workers
- Taking rat tails to Mumias

The meeting ended in disarray. After the disagreements Anyiri Kosando (the grandfather of Nick Ogola of Maseno University) ululated very sharply calling on the Uyoma warriors, "*Since* when did Uyoma men grind for men like them?" *Nyaka kara ango' mane chwuo Uyoma orego ne chwuo wete gi*? Oyuga Wuon Aloo woke up and caned the horse that Hobly had mounted. Opondo ja Kotwal knocked sample of the Queens crown from Hobly's head. Otieno Osogo caned Odera Ulalo with a rod. Mr.C.W Hobly got annoyed and hit Otieno Osogo with the butt of the gun and hell broke loose. Hobly and his entourage dispersed unceremoniously leaving the meeting in a huff They promised a return match with the defiant Uyoma.

Upon their return to Mumias the Provincial Headquaters an urgent meeting was held under the Chairmanship of Mumia Ashiundu. The meeting discussed the arrogance of the Uyoma people and the embarrassment it caused Mr. Hobly the Provincial Commissioner and British Administration at large. During the meeting Mumia Ashiundu told the gathering that the uncouth behavior is not new to them. "We lived with them and this kind of arrogance is the reason why we chased them away from our land. These are our very close relatives and we know them very well. Only military expedition on them can bear fruits". The meeting was adjorned and Odera Ulalo was given the task to mobilize an armed operation from the collaborating communities to attack Uyoma.

THE MUMBO MASSACRE UNMASKED

In the morning of 26th December 1899 Odera Ulalo led the Uyoma armed operation, the operation started at Likungu, Manyuanda Centre. The military operation involved killing, looting, raping and burning of homesteads. Many women, children and oldmen were beaten, injured and killed, among those who were killed were Monye Ogungo wuon Oyola who was shot while atop a tree, on the same trail Chiama also met his death. Now the operation headed towards Mboga's home who was accused of not having convinced the Uyoma people to collaborate with the white administration yet he had cheated Mumia Ashiundu that he had convinced the Uyoma people into collaboration and submission to the British rule. Mboga in his smartness abandoned his home with his family and boarded his boats towards Mbita. When the operation reached Mboga's home they vented their anger and burned the whole homestead to ashes. Mboga with his family watched his home burning while sailing towards Mbita to his maternal uncles home for refuge.

In the morning of 27th December 1899 the whole of Uyoma was in turmoil and many people ran for refuge to their other leader OLuoch Abaki whom they thought would not be attacked since he was related to the Gem people through marital status, his eldest wife Abul Nya Gina was from Gem. Others escaped by boats towards karachuonyo, Homa Bay and Chula Rabuor.

Ayoro Gwela from Asembo advised Jo-Uyoma to seek refuge at OLuoch Abaki's home. OLuoch was working as an orderly of Mumias, The reason for him advising them to do this was because one of OLuoch's wives come from Gem. He is the grandfather of Akelo Gwela the former chairman of Bondo County Council.

There is no armour against fate, incidentally, His advice did not surfice. The military operation reached OLuoch Abaki's home and the home was surrounded. Meanwhile OLuoch Abaki moved out of the home in surrender carrying his hands up and holding twigs as the Luo normal sign of peace, as the assumed Uyoma leader and the owner of the homestead where people had gathered OLuoch moved in a friendly majestical style towards Odera Ulalo. Odera Ulalo's soldiers were ordered to gun down OLuoch Abaki and shoot Jo-Uyoma indiscriminately.OLuoch Abaki died in cold blood without uttering a word, he fell head on to the ground and those in the home could not believe the macabre scene and hell broke lose. People ran helter skelter bullets were sprayed everywhere and anywhere, the Uyoma people died enmasse, many were injured and maimed. The notable Uyoma warriors who blantly faced the guns were; Oluga Dipondo, Ogundo Ragwar,Ogundo Liech, Malago Pacho Kombe, Monye and Ogutu Anyieche the prophesised child by Ogalo Wuon Tieng'o *Jabilo*.

The Odera Ulalo group captured several young women and took with them grains and livestock. The Uyoma people were very angry on that day, they regrouped and gathered momentum. They agreed unanimously that there was no way that their livestock and women could be taken by these intruders. Otieno Osogo and Molo Nyadundo led the Uyoma warriors to recapture their livestock and women. They followed the intruders from OLuoch Abaki's home in Lieta and caught up with them between Mituri and Migowa. As the warriors faced the intruders the fighting ensued and many fighters from both sides were injured and in the process of the fracas Molo Nyadundo was shot on the knee from behind by Odera Ulalo. At this point he was just about to spear a white man on the horse. This motivated the Uyoma warriors to keep up the fight. Molo kept on fighting while limping and bleeding profusely. Molo together with the other Uyoma warriors managed to salvage more than half of the looted livestock.The approximate number of livestock taken was over 4000 but the Uyoma gladiators managed to capture more than 50% of the captured livestock. All the women were saved by the attack which made them scatter and escape during fighting confusion and they all returned home safely.

On their return home, the injured Molo bleeding and limping collapsed and died at Migowa next to the Onyango Olot's home. While dying in the presence of the other warriors Molo said, "We have fought a heavy battle and taught the white man and their henchmen a lesson and Uyoma should never surrender".that was the battle of guns versus spears. *Ka chuny Molo pok ochot, nowachone jowadgi ni ' Kawuono wasekedo lweny mapek kendo wapuonjo wagunda go kod andhokego kik Uyoma yienegi gikaw piny magilokwa wasumbni'*.Mano lweny mar jobunde gi jo tonge. This is the climax of the historical Mumbo massacre by the Whiteman in Uyoma. This marks the beginning of the freedom fight against the white domination in Uyoma and Kenya.

Uyoma day is marked and celebrated on every 27th of December to commemorate and celebrate the Mumbo Massacre and the Uyoma heroes.

It was the spilling of this Uyoma blood that watered the seed for freedom fighting, it ignited and politicised Jo-Uyoma.The following are the notable freedom fighters; Jonathan Okwiri, Nathan Ojungo, Walter Fanuel Odede, Ramogi Achieng Oneko, D. O. Makasembo, and Mbogo Okello woud Mandera among others. It is in this vain and bitterness that they joined other Freedom fighters like Harry Thuku, Jomo Kenyatta and the rest of Kenya.

Fifty two years later, the same statement was echoed in Ruringu stadium in Nyeri by Ramogi Achieng' Oneko that *"the tree of freedom is watered by blood"* and hence the declaration of MAU MAU and the state of emergency in Kenya in 1952.

ESTABLISHMENT OF BRITISH RULE IN UYOMA

After the Mumbo Massacre the Uyoma people were left tongue-tied and were now at the mercy of the British Empire known as the great 'British Empire where the sun never sets.' They agreed to collaborate like their neighbors, but they remained suspicious of the British rule. *Uyoma noyie tege.* They actually never wanted to be given a leader *jatelo* the way their neighbors' leaders were hand-picked by the White people and their cronies. They always argued that they had their long list of outstanding leaders accepted by the community since their settlement from Kanyamwa.

The first traditional Chief or Leader of Jo Uyoma as they settled after the Kanyamwa expedition was Oguta Wauga from Katweng'a of Kawuor family, this family has produced several chiefs and leaders such as Otumba, Ojungo, Onditi Achola, Dan Okuma, Henry Ouko Otieno and other leaders such as Apollo Washington Juma Otito, Hon. Reuben Ndolo former MP in Nairobi among others.

The second traditional Chief was Oginga Agidhi from Katweng'a clan. He was instrumental in the expulsion of the Kale people from Uyoma.

The third traditional Chief was Mboga wuon Otieno, comes from Kobor family in Kokwiri. He was connected with Slave Traders from Uganda; he was suspected to have brought tsetse fly *Maugo* from Uganda which was very plenty in Uyoma and magic *bilo*. He had good rapport and linkages with neighbors as far as Buganda Kingdom. He predicted the coming of the Whiteman to Uyoma.

Haya Ngode was from Kochieng family of Kabudha Naya of South Uyoma. He succeeded Mboga as the fifth traditional Chief in the process of the establishment of the Whiteman's rule. During his reign he established and installed his Assistants *Mirukni/Miruka* from every clan in Uyoma, he used the delegating management method through his Assistants. This made him an efficient, effective and successful Chief *Ruoth*. Among the various Assistants was Otumba Mbede from Katweng'a.

The Provincial Commissioner of Eastern Uganda, Mr.C.W Hobly *Obilo* was instructed to formerly install all Traditional Chiefs from all Collaborating communities in his Province. In this regard, messengers were sent to all the Chiefs to assemble for formal installation in Mumias, the Provincial headquater of Eastern Uganda on 5th January 1900. One such messenger arrived in Uyoma on the 3rd of January 1900, to deliver the message to Haya Ngode who was the Traditional Chief of Uyoma. He reached Chianda and was taken to Otumba Mbede's home who was Haya Ngode's Assistant *miruka*. On arrival at the home, he was warmly welcomed by the family and Otumba himself. He was fed and given accommodation. He narrated his mission to Otumba who told him that Haya's home is a long distant away and he could not reach the place that day in the late hour. He told the messenger that he would make arrangements the next day for the message to reach Haya Ngode. On the very evening Otumba consulted a handful of advisors from his katweng'a clan who told him to go to Mumias and represent Jo-Uyoma. His advisors told him that this was a golden chance to become chief *Hawi olwar e lweti.* The next morning Otumba asked the messenger to go back as he had sent the message to Haya.

On 5th January 1900 during the formal installations of Chiefs in Mumias, Haya Ngode's name was read three times with no reponse, in the process a bulky black well built man from Uyoma strolled majestically to the dias claiming that he was the anointed Chief by Jo-Uyoma. He reported that Haya Ngode had rejected the invitation because of the Mumbo massacre. He was then asked if he was ready to be installed as the substantive Chief of Uyoma. He replied that he was ready but requested that the installation should be carried out in Uyoma. Hobly the Provincial Commissioner and Chief Guest obliged. The following chiefs were installed Ondu of Kisumu, Odera Ulalo of Gem, Noyi of Seme, Okwako of Ugenya, Aenda of Alego, Adhola of Asembo and Ondiek wuon Auko *Bunde Kamnara* of Sakwa, Kitoto of Kano among others.

On 26th January 1900 the Provincial Commissioner Mr.C.W Hobly came to Uyoma for the installation ceremony. Many people attended this ceremony and Haya Ngode was also present. Before this ceremony Haya Ngode had been warned by Otumba not to talk in that ceremony because the Provincial Office had installed somebody else as the Chief. After Otumba was installed as the Chief of Uyoma, he was then asked to make a maiden speech. One of the major things he said in conclusion was that, "From this day onwards Haya Ngode and his family are under home arrest, but the Uyoma people will cultivate, plant, weed and harvest for him". He then ended his speech greeted the Provincial Commissioner and the meeting ended. *Kochakore Kawuono Haya wuon Ngode ok Oyiene wuok e dalane kod joge……… JoUyoma biro puro, doyo kendo Keyone .Omoso PC bang'e bura norumo.*

Chief Otumba Mbede during his Chieftainship organized and formalized the boundaries between Uyoma and Asembo, and regulated the disputed boundaries between Katweng'a and Kobong'. The long disputed boundary between Uyoma and Sakwa was harmonized. He encouraged the Anglican Missionaries to establish Churches and Schools in Uyoma despite Uyoma peoples' resistance to the Whiteman's religion which according to Jo–Uyoma included Christianity and Islam. Otumba encouraged Jo- Uyoma to embrace christianty.He initiated the construction of the 1st church which is St. Peter's Chianda Anglican Church and later Chianda sector which is now known as Chianda Primary School. He sent the first batch of students to the historic Maseno School. Some of the students who attended Maseno School from 1906 were; Musa Outa, James Sigar, John Mark Yongo, Bwana Ong'injo, Jonathan Okwiri and Jacob Orwa among others. He introduced the planting of sisal and cultivation and groundnuts. He worked from1900- 1917 and died in 1945.

Chief Moi Okweso took over from Chief Otumba Mbede; he was from Kokwiri of West Uyoma. He was instrumental in child education and construction of roads, the well known road is the one from Nyakongo to Owimbi. He ruled from 1917 to1922 before going into exile in South Nyanza because he could not bear the embarrassment caused to him by some of his officers, one mr. Sigar who had collected mononey for purchase of instruments but failed to keep records and embezzled the funds collected. Moi had also to flee because of the boat tragedy that capsized while with his subjects on a visit to South Nyanza.

Chief Moi was succeeded by Nathan Ojungo Otumba from Katweng'a who was also the son of Ex-Chief Otumba Mbede. He encouraged education in Uyoma and was also the beneficiary of Missionary education in Maseno. He also introduced and participated in football and athletics in Uyoma, also improved relationship between the communities in Uyoma particularly between Katweng'a and Kokwiri when he appointed Eliazar Oswago as his tax clerk/ secretary.He did so because he wanted to appease the Kokwiri clan where his predessessor had come from. He ruled for eighteen years until 1940

Chief Jonathan Okwiri Nyakinya was from Kotwal Kobong', he was a student from Maseno School and later became a teacher at Chianda Sector School and a headteacher at Government African School in Kisumu which is currently Kisumu Boys High School. He took over from Ex-Chief Ojungo.

Chief Jonathan Okwiri was a student of Maseno and he is always remembered for keeping time especially during meetings *Barazas*. One such occassion was when one white Provincial Commisioner Mr.C.H.Williams organized for a meeting with Jo-Uyoma at Owimbi at 10.00 o'clock but arrived at the venue for the meeting later at 3 o'clock and found that the assembly was already dispersed by the Chief. When the PC demanded to know why people had left the meeting, the Chief castigated him and told him, "If you are the makers of the watch then you should be the first to keep time, *Ka un ema uloso saa to in emaonego ikuong rito saa*". He cherished family harmony and encouraged peaceful relationship between husband and wife and would intervene whenever there were signs of divorce. He encouraged modern education having been a Maseno student.He loathed laziness and you could not approach him with nonsense.He retired in protest against the arrest and detention of his former pupils at Maseno School by the British colonial Government in 1952,the said pupils were Walter Fanuel Odede and Ramogi Achieng' Oneko.

After his resignation as the chief, he turned his energy into political activism, through his school and Civil Service networks he mobilized many like-minded people to agitate against the Colonial government. He worked with senior Luo personalities such as, Ex-Chief Nathan Ojungo, Ogude Wuon Nyaoro, Isaiah Ndisi from Uyoma, Ex-Chief Paul Mbuya from Karachuonyo, Elijah Bonyo from Sakwa, and Omino Ogola from Kisumu among others from the larger Luo Communities.

Their informal political vehicle was known as *Piny Owacho* the people have said, whose first conference was held at Lundha Gem in 1922. The leadership of this group was: Chairman Jonathan Ojungo Otumba, Secretary was Jonathan Okwiri, Assistant Secretary Joel Omino Ogola, and Treasurer Paul Mbuya wuod Akoko. Joel Omino Ogola was a clerk in the DCs Office in Kisumu; he was very happy with the idea and strongly supported and organized the meeting venue in his rural home, a dangerous assignment for a Government Officer at that time. During this time all their meeting resolutions were given to a young man by the name Achieng' Oneko from Uyoma, who disseminated the information through his newspaper called Ramogi.

The officials mainly from Uyoma, Jonathan Okwiri and Jonathan Ojungo Otumba approached various leaders to join this movement against the white domination. The notable visits were one to Amoth Wuon Owira in Alego, Odera Akang"o from Gem and Nindo KaNyangaga from Seme among others. They all rejected the request on grounds that the Uyoma people are known to be mischievious and defiant to authority. This was in reference to the historical mischief of Jo-Uyoma while in Alego from Kawango. *Amoth Kowira ne oduokogi 'JoUyoma kaka ne ugoyo wa ka un Alego ka ua Kawango, kendo udwaro keto wa echandruok"*. They also approached Oginga Odinga from Sakwa and a teacher in the famous Maseno School, Odinga rejected their request and told them that, leave this uncalled for movement it will bring turmoil, the white man will kill very many people and that the Whiteman will leave on his own. *Oginga Odinga ne oduoko gi,'Ni mondo jorotenge owere kod jowasungu, nikech wasungu richo biro negogi, kendo biro kelo koko mang'eny, chieng' moro gini wuog kendgi"*. Later on in history the same Oginga Odinga made a great turn around and led Kenyans to fight for freedom.

When Ongalo Oneko approached his father Oneko Nyauchi to air his view on his son Achieng's activities on this mission, the old Oneko Nyauchi replied just let him go and knock one day they will open for them. *Kane openji ni gima Achieng' gini timo ni donge biro kelo tho, kwer wuodi. To en ne oduoko gidhi giduon'g aduonga' chieng'moro noyawnegi.*

The objectives of this group were as follows: The Whiteman to leave Kenya, removal of taxation and kipande system, equal education system for Europeans, Indians and Africans, equal empolyment opportunities, wages and the establishment of the Luo nation.

During this time the Kikuyu community was also agitating for the same issues apart from occupation of their land. The Kikuyu group was led by Harry Thuku and Eliud Mathu among others.

At this time Achieng Oneko was publishing a news paper known as Ramogi articulating the Luo and Kikuyu agitations against the Whiteman's colonialism.

Achieng Oneko brought the two groups together so that they could speak with one voice. The leaders that represented the two sides were Jonathan Okwiri, Jonathan Ojungo Otumba from the Luo group, Harry Thuku and Eliud Mathu from the Kikuyu group. The moderator of this meeting was Achieng Oneko. One of the outcomes of this historic meeting was that they should hold periodic meetings and bring on board the other tribes. Achieng Oneko being a young man was mandated to mobilize and created linkages with other tribes. The other tribes that were approached were the baluhia and it started off with Kawango, where he knew he would get soft landing because Wango, the patriarch of Kawango is brother to Omia Ramul, the patriarch of Uyoma.

Later on Kenya African Union (KAU) was formed to become a Kenyan inclusive party. The Leadership was as follows, Harry Thuku as Chairman, Achieng' Oneko as the Secretary and Mzau Mwimi as the Treasurer.

After the arrest of Harry Thuku and Mzau Mwimi, Jomo Kenyatta became the Chairman, Achieng' Oneko remained Secretary and Paul Ngei as Treasurer. The other active members were Bildad Kaggia, Kungu Karumba and Fred Kubai.

After the declaration of the state of emergency,Kenya remained in a political lull for two years but it is important to note that Walter Fanuel Odede from Uyoma became the acting President of KAU after the detention of Jomo Kenyatta, Achieng' Oneko, Bildad Kaggia, Paul Ngei, Kungu Karumba and Fred Kubai.

On the 21st October, Walter Fanuel Odede from Uyoma took over the Chairmanship of KAU assisted by W.W. Awori as the Secretary General of the party.

Walter Fanuel Odede travelled to Britain to seek legal expertise who could represent the Kapenguria Six. He got a Queen's Counsel by the name D.N. Pritt. It is recorded in history that D.N.Pritt Q.C. successfully won the case; the Kapenguria Six were released and later detained the same day. On 30th April 1953 Walter Fanuel Odede was arrested and detained and by June 1953 KAU was prescribed. Walter Fanuel Odede was detained until 1960. During this period African political associations were not allowed to operate but it is interesting to note that the educated elite from Nyanza were already getting involved in National politics.

In 1954 the Lyttleton constitution allowed for the formation of a multi- racial council of ministers.This led to the appointment of B.A Ohanga another educated elite from Nyanza the Minister for Community Development .It was the appointment of Honourable Ohanga that sparked political rivalry amongst the elites in Nyanza. On one hand,there were those like Ohanga who embraced the concept on multi –

racialism' and on the other hand, there were those like Odinga who strongly opposed multi-racialism; Mr. Ohanga was particularly censured by this group for accepting nomination to the Legistlative Council in place of Mr.Odede.

After the publication of the Legistlative Council on *African Representation* ordinance in 1956. It became eminent that a General Election would take place in 1957, this ignited the activities of African District Association. It became apparent that Oginga Odinga would oppose B .A. Ohanga incidentally at this point Oginga Odinga had risen to the rank of chairman *ker* of the giant Luo union which gave him political clout.

Prior to the election of the Legislative Governing Council (LEGCO), some Central Nyanza candidates met under the Chairmanship of Vitalis Asugo from Uyoma. These politicians included Richard Arina D C, and Odindo Nyasaka from Uyoma, B. A. Ohanga from Gem, and Oginga Odinga from Sakwa. The Uyoma aspirants rallied behind Oginga Odinga and he beat B.A. Ohanga in the elections. This marked the beginnings of Odinga's rise to political supremacy.

Agitations for Kenyan independence intensified with notable incidences which are memorable. There were many incidences in Kenya demanding for Kenya's independence from the colonial rule. One such incident took place in Kisumu known as the naked demonstration against the British Government to give Kenya her independence, release the political detainees and allow the activists to wear their red party uniforms. The activists stripped naked in the streets of Kisumu from *Chiro Mbero* towards the DCs Offices, where they were surounded and arrested. The ring leader was the notorious Mbogo Okelo from Uyoma known for stripping naked. Mbogo Okelo had turned to be the modern notorious Omolo Ngo'ngo'. The following political activists participated; from Uyoma Abonyo wuon Oyombe, Omil Koka Kola, Otuoma wuon Ooro (Abila), Richard Ochido Alindi *Ochido Macharia, Onyango Radier* and Mariko Odipo. The other representatives from other places were: Owino Abuoro, Omolo Arambe and Were Olonde from Nyakach; From kano Ombok Thim, Ywaya Odero from Asembo, Naam Akumu from Alego, Owuor ka Maondo from Yimbo, Rasamba from Manyala, Zedi Kobiero Olenyo ja Matangwe from Sakwa among others. The woman who carried their clothes was Odundo nyar Ouma from Uyoma.

Their demonstration song was as follows:

Mbogo son of Okelo without you Kenya remains empty

Mbogo son of Okelo without you Nyanza remains empty

Mbogo son of Okelo without you Luo remains empty

Mbogo wuon Okelo ki ionge to dala Kenya odong' nono

Mbogo wuon Okelo ki ionge to dala Nyanza odong' nono

Mbogo wuon Okelo ki ionge to dala Luo odong' nono

These demonstrators were arrested and taken to Court the next day naked, interestingly other naked demonstrators arrived at the Court; they were also arrested for contempt of Court. Their message to the

DC Mr. Padressor was that if the Government could not allow the youth actitvists to wear their KANU red uniforms then they would walk naked in Kisumu and other towns.

Chieng'no ema ne yawuot Luo mangeny ogonyore mowuotho duge kochakore chiro mbero nyaka ka DC kendo kinyne gi donjo e kot duge.Mbogo emanotelo ne gi.

When this issue reached the DC Mr. Padressor, he instructed immediate release of the demonstrators as this would be an embarrassment to the Queen of England before the International community. This would beat the whole purpose of British and European objective of colonization and taking civilization to Africa.

During the struggle and agitation for independence some of the Uyoma people featured prominently in the KANU party structure at the regional and National levels.They were ; Mbogo Wuon Okello, Dickson Oruko Makasembo,Jonathan Ojungo Otumba, Jonathan Okwiri Nyakinya, Walter Odede and Ramogi Achieng Oneko. Walter Fanuel Odede was the Chairman of KANU in Siaya and later Chairman of Luo Union Movement (LUM).

Prior to the Kenyan independence, several young people were admitted with the assistance of Ramogi Achieng Oneko, Tom Mboya and Oginga Odinga to various academic institutions In Europe, USA and other foreign Countries to replace the British and other foreigners in Government and even Private sector. The scholars from Uyoma who went for studies abroad and returned to take up Senior employment positions were, Dr. Wera Ambitho , Walter Nyawanda Ajugu, Awando Jagongo, Ong'iro Ka-Ong'iro ,Ouko Jotham, Dr.Ongong'a Achieng, Dr. Olola Oneko ,Ayieko Omolo, Obara, Onyango Radier among others. The above individuals from Uyoma went for studies through the efforts of Hon. Ramogi Achieng Oneko.

At the dawn of independence several Uyoma people were included in the formation of the first Govrnment headed by Mzee Jomo Kenyatta with the Vice President Jaramogi Oginga Odinga.

Hon Ramogi Achieng Oneko became the MP for Nakuru Constituency and the first Cabinet Minister for Information, Broadcasting and Tourism and wildlife, Dickson Oruko Makasembo became the Senator of Central Nyanza, Justus OLuoch Adel became the Permanent Secrtary Ministry of Public Works, Meshack Okelo Ndisi became the Permanent Secretary Ministry of Labour, Richard Arina Oulo was a DC.

The story and expedition of the Uyoma people in Kenya spans over a period of 14 generations and for approximately 500 years.

The generations span from 15th to 21st Century starting with Ramogi Ajuang (II) to Lwande Oneko the author of this book. The majority of these people, i.e over 90% were born and buried in their ancestral land Uyoma even with the migrations. Jo-Uyoma have lived in the present day Uyoma for 14 generations. Apart from the name of Odhiriany and Otimbla all the other names are very common in Uyoma todate. You will find many people with the name Ramogi, Owila, Osewe, Ojal, Otonde, Were and the name Omia in Asembo and in Kawango it is Mumia

TURMOILS IN UYOMA

Jo-Uyoma faced many turbulances but there are turmoils that are documented here. These upheavals have had negative and positive impact on the wellbeing of Jo-Uyoma. Some of the turmoils range from famine and inadequate grazing land, hinderance to the watering point in Uyoma, Badblood and sibling wrangles in Kawango, Worldwar I and II, the return from Kanyamwa and the hectic entry back to the ancestral land. The Mumbo massacre, the first and second Invasion of Majoni in Uyoma in 1960 and 1972 respectively. The removal of the District Headquarters from Madiany *Thurmony* the symbol of the ancestral land and the burial site of the Uyoma patriarchs both Omia Ramul and Owila.

Before we look at the turmoils listed above, it would prudent to make a summary of the femines that have caused distressful situations in Uyoma. In the last two centuries the following are the list of femine in Uyoma:

Between 1870 to 1871, there was *Ke-angieng laki* because Uyoma people had not planted after migrating from Kanyamwa.

In 1889 there was an outbreak of rinderpest that spread like wild fire over the whole of East Africa reaching Tanganyika towards the end of 1890. There was also terrible famine called *Ke' ongong'a*. Most of the people in Luo Nyanza were named after this famine.

1890 – 1907 the Rinder Pest disease and famine known in Luo as *Ke' Apamo*. The disease affected the whole of Nile valley killed livestock in thousands especially cattle. This disease was brought by livestock bought in Russia and other Black sea Ports. The disease was followed by the outbreak of anthrax *yamo* which attacked the remaining livestock. threatening to destroy utterly the livestock economy. The disease devastated the place known as Lela near Maseno and it was nicked named the livestock grave yard *Lienddhok*.

In 1890s sleeping sickness engulfed the Lake Basin Region. Sleeping sickness is a tropical disease carried by tsetsefly that causes uncalled sleep and it causes death. It broke out on the Eastern shores of Lake Victoria starting Busoga District in Eastern Uganda and then spread into Samia, Bunyala, ~~Imbo~~ Yimbo, Sakwa then into Uyoma. There was a rumour that it was brought by Mboga Otieno and Ose Ongogo the father of Owenda *akonyi to ok nenni* these two gentlemen were frequent visitors to Buganda. It is said they brought the insect in guards *puga* a long Utonga in Sakwa, Likungu, Osindo, Misori, Kasiri, Kogonga and Adola, Kanyada, Gwasi, Lambwe, Karungu and Kadem in South Nyanza.

The disease was devastating that those people who were living near the lakeshore were advised to move away from the lakeshore. Thousands of people died as a result of this pandemic.

A song was composed to signify the effect of the disease.

I spent a night down the Lake

I was bitten thoroughly by mosquitoes and tsetsefies

I spend a night at Kadimo Lowland

I was thoroughly bitten by Mosquitos and tsetseflies

Down in Yimbo, down at Kadimo

I was thoroughly bitten by Mosquitoes and tsetseflies

Anindo mwalo

Suna kayo ng'eya

Amindo mwalo kadimo mwalo

Suna kayo ng'eya, suna gi Maugo

Kadimo, kadimo

Suna kayo ng'eya

Yimbo mwalo, kadimo mwalo

Suna kayo ng'eya suna gi maugo

Suna kayo ng'eya

Between1890 to 1907 there was famine nicknamed Ke *Odila* that killed many people; it mainly affected the shores of Lake Victoria.

Between 1917 to1918 there was *Kanga* famine. Most of the people were named after this devastating famine, the famine was named after the introduction of tribal police known as Kanga.

Between 1928 to 1932 there was *Ke-Otuoma*; this famine was caused by raiding locusts in the Lake Region that ravaged not only the farms but also the vegetation

1943 – 1944 *Ke – otonglo* it was called the ten cents piece because of the shortage of food and inflation there of meant that the smallest unit of money accepted in the market went from the two- cent piece upto the ten cent piece.

The ten cent famine effect lingered on over and even after the end of the World War II in 1945

Between 1951 to 1952 there was *Arong'a* famine *ke- Arong'a*. This famine was characterized by torrential and devastating rainfall that destroyed and wiped out crops in two major seasons.

1961 – 1963 there was indepent rainfall *kodh Uhuru* where crops were swept by the floods only African potatoes could be harvested by wading ~~from~~ through the Waters.

The years 1980 and 2009 were characterized with draught that caused very poor harvest and it also wiped livestock in thousands.

The lessons learnt from famine, draught and livestock destruction seems to be the rationale the irrigation enterprise that is currently being practiced along the lake shores of Uyoma.

WORLD WAR I AND II

The World War One took place between 1914 to 1918 while World War Two took place between 1939 to 1945. The War brought destruction to the World in regard to loss of human lives, it is estimated that over 8.5 million military and civilians lost their lives in World War One. More than 71 million millitary and civilian deaths, in World War Two. Apart from human lives lost there was a great deal of loss of property, even in places where there was no war.

The World Wars were negative in many ways but in Uyoma and elsewhere there were some positive impact that promoted education and economic development.

In Luo land by 1900, the Luo chief Odera, Akang'o was providing 1,500 porters for a British expedition against the Nandi who were opposed to the construction of the Railway Line. This contribution towards the Colonial domination and the building of the Railway line, dubbed *the Lunatic line* in the British Parliament was incidentally the seeds of Luo Education dominance in Africa.

In 1915 due to many favors he had given the Colonial Government, this Government wanted to use him to influence the Luo community to support the Colonial initiatives. And so, the Colonial Government sent *Odera Akang'o*, the *ruoth* of Gem, to Kampala. Uganda. He was impressed by the British settlement there and upon his return home he initiated a forced process of adopting western lifestyles. This resulted in the rapid education of the **Luo** in the English language and English ways. This visit turned out to be the beginnings of the greatest Luo Capacity building venture that will live time memorial as Africa's household of academic excellence. This influence spread all over Luo land and Uyoma was not left out. Incidentally he also initiated afforestation in Gem and it spread into Luoland.

The Colonial Government recruited many Africans in the British War with the Germans, known as World War I, a War Africans never understood.

Those gallant soldiers that were recruited participated in World War One and Two in any position were exposed to the Worldly experiences beyond their native abode and they brought many new ideas, skills and knowledge in Uyoma and Kenya at large.

Those who went to World War One were instrumental in the promotion of Education, Religion especially Christianity and overall economic development in Uyoma. They learnt some English and Kiswahili during their interactions with the British and Kenyans from other tribes. The most popular language among the Africans was Kiswahili and English was the War language. All Jo-Uyoma who went to World War One took their children to School. Those who went to the War were able to get employment in the Colonial Government administrative system. Since they went to War they were more trusted by the British Government. In the process these people learnt many European ways of life such as meals, etiquate, clothing, vehicle repairs. They gained economic power from the salaries they got from the employment. The places where most Africans got employment were, the Colonial Government Administration, the armed forces or the uniformed forces, the railways, the European farms among others. They also became religious leaders, mostly Christians but even Muslims.

The notable personalities who came back and made impact were such people as:

Oyieko Obuya took all his children to schools and professional fields. His offsprings the famous teacher George White Obala of Okela, Okecha from Kabuong' also took all his offsprings to school and some of the offsprings are Walter maguke and Omori Maguke.

Oneko Nyauchi from kabudha took all his offsprings to school, notably plus all his daughters. Most of his grandchildren are University graduates he is the father of Ramogi AchiengOneko.

Harun Njago from Katwenga' took all his children to school and most of his grandchildren acquired University education.

Ndolo Oluga was appointed as the representative of Uyoma in the African Advisory Council in 1920; one of his sons was a permanent Secretary in the Tanzanian Government and one of his grandsons Reuben Ndolo was an MP in Nairobi.

Those who went to World War Two came back with many ideas and were Colonial Government employees. Incidentally many came back with negative ideologies against the British Colonial rule. They took lead in agitation for self rule which meant Kenya's independence; they joined political, labour and social movements which were anti Colonial rule. Many of them became anti Christian, some of them followed Jaramogi Oginga Odinga and Ramogi Achieng Oneko in dropping Christian names. Odinga dropped the name Adonija and replaced it with Jaramogi; Achieng Oneko dropped the name Richard and took the name Ramogi. Jomo Kenyatta dropped the name Johnstone Kamau. In Uyoma Ogot Kogot was known for his anti Colonial activities after service during the war. Oruko Makasembo became a political activist after serving during the war and later rose to the rank of a Senator.

After the war Josephat Ogola became an Assistant Chief of Kobong'. Ogundo Arunda was employed in the armed or uniformed forces; he is the father of the Unionist and Ex-Councillor of Nairobi Ochino Ogundo.

The impact of the World Wars had similarity in regard to the promotion of education, employment and overall economic development.

THE 1st INVASION OF MAJONI OF 1960

The Colonial Government had a strong hold in Nyanza with great hope for support compared to Central Kenya which was dominated by the notorious MAU MAU terrorists from the Kikuyu tribesmen. The second most populated area in Kenya with many educated people with Government positions and schools was Nyanza. This geographical area covered three major tribes led by Luo followed by Baluhya and Kisii plus the minority Kuria who were in Kenya and Tanganyika. During the MAU MAU terrorist struggle for Kenya's independence, the Colonial Government made social development in the loyal zones such as the Coastal zone, Eastern and Northen Kenya.

The only place that made the Government uneasy was Uyoma apart from the obvious urban centres such as Kisumu, Kisii, kakamega and the boarder towns of Busia and Isbania. The urban centres were populated with educated and enlightened Kenyas who agitated for independence, the border towns had an additional neighbor influence and that is Busia with Uganda influence, while Namanga and Isbania had the notorious Mwalimu Julius Kabarage Nyerere's influence from Tanganyika.

The Central Nyanza District Commissiner, Mr. Padressa and the Bondo District Officer, Isaac Okwiri OLuoch and the Chief Elijah OLuoch Atipa in their normal duties were on duty of responding to the Uyoma domestic demonstrations in their territory urging people to defy the Colonial Government through the KANU activists. The KANU leaders from Uyoma were many. They had been influenced by Jonathan Okwiri, a former Chief who had resigned unceremoniously, the rogue Nyanza KANU Chairman none other than Dickson Oruko Makasembo. The worst influence was the detention of Fanuel Odede who had taken Jomo Kenyatta's position as KAU Chairman and as such was associated to MAU MAU. To add salt to the wound was the detention and the role played by Ramogi Achieng Oneko who was black listed as a MAU MAU terrorist who ignited and fuelled anti-Government activities not only in Nyanza but in Kenya.

The Central Nyanza DC, the DO and Uyoma Chief called a special baraza (meeting) to quell the possible uprise from this interior zone. They came prepared for a confrontation based on bad Colonial historical records.

The meeting was set for 10.00 a.m. and the DC was literally shocked to find Jo-Uyoma seated, the time keeping was influenced by the former Chief Jonathan Okwiri. The meeting was well attended; after the introductions the DC took the stage narrated the Government achievements in regard to increased number of schools that promotes the desired education, the Missionary efforts that have brought Christianity which promoted a God loving community, the development of roads and infrastracture that promotes economic development.

The DC praised the people of Nyanza for their loyalty to the Colonial Government whose effort is to promote political stability and peace in the Country, before he could continue the Uyoma Chief Uhuru, Mr. Dickson Mbogo Okello interrupted the DC and told him that the Colonial Government should not expect peace if Achieng Oneko was still languishing in prison. The DC quickly replied that Oneko would be released in good time the way Odede was released afew months earlier. Mbogo replied in furry that the DC had to know that the Whiteman's time was going and Kenya would get its independence. While the DC and Mbogo were fuming at each other a KANU activist Akoko wuod Okwiri asked for a point of order which was granted by the DO to divert attention and then Akoko spoke in excellent English following Mbogo's foot steps and he said the following, "Bwana DO I wish to bring to your attention to a point of order, is it in order for a young junior boy like this Whiteman to smoke a pipe infront of adults during the process of such an important meeting?" He added "this is total disrespect". The DO stood up and ordered for the immediate arrest of Akoko. As the policemen moved towards Akoko the meeting attendants immediately build a human shield around Akoko giving him enough time to run and escape which he did as the crowd cheered. They all sung the freedom song. Meanwhile the DO's attention was drawn towards Mbogo who defiantely laughed loudly to the top of his voice. The police jumped on Mbogo before the crowd could shield him, quick police action made Mbogo find himself in a Police van and to Bondo Police Station and thereafter Kisumu at Kodiaga Prison without going to Court. The meeting ended unceremoniously, as the Chief shouted "*Jo-Dalawa utugo kich, Ombogo ja rachar biro hinyowa*" *(*My people you have rattled the bees, the Whiteman will unleash terror upon us). The DO shouted and said "*Bura orumo to ubiro ng'eyo ni an Okwiri Jusa ma Ja-Gem kendo ubiro ng'eyo teko Ja-Rachar*" (The meeting has ended but you will know that I am

Okwiri from Gem and the strength and might of the Whiteman). The meeting surely ended and Jo-Uyoma replied the DO and his DC *"Jo-Gem gi Jo-Rochere ok nyal buogo Jo-Uyoma"* (The people of Gem and a Whiteman cannot threaten Jo-Uyoma).

The DC, the DO and the Chief drove directly to Bondo and later to Kisumu.

The next day three lorries loaded with Majoni (General Service Unit) drove into Uyoma and took strategy positions. One group moved from Aram to Lwanda Kotieno, the second group was stationed at Kunya (the hot spot and Mbogo's home) and the third group was stationed at Ruma next to Odede's home and the main narrow entrance to Uyoma.

In every corner of Uyoma Jo-Uyoma men *nogweyo* chanted *Jowi Jowi, KanyaLuo, kanyaLuo, aero kut oruko kutoruko* as the women ululated to motivate the men to fight Majoni. Jo-Uyoma came in full swing with spears with shields, Bows and arrows, clubs and sticks. They confronted and fought the Majoni and the three Lorries of Majoni retreated to Bondo after two grueling days and the Uyoma men gallantly fighting back in defence. Several men were injured and maimed. Majoni retreated with many of them also injured

On the third day the Majoni got a back up from Kisumu and regrouped they unleashed terror on Uyoma. They asked people to produce Kipande, Bicycle licence, tax receipt and a dusk to dawn curfew was impossed. The day light meant thorough beating with clubs and caning with lashes. The men met the wrath of the Whiteman as promised but on a very sad note many women were beaten and raped, the thuggery went on for seven consecutive days. When the Government heard this incident the Authorities ordered immediate redeployment of the Majoni. The terror on Uyoma was stopped; many people died later out of injuries inflicted on them by the Colonial Government.

The incident shook the colonial administration, Sir. Patrick Renison the Governor reshuffled the provincial administration, Mr. Padressa was transferred outside Nyanza, Isaac Okwiri promoted to full D.C. a white District Officer Mr. Johnson was posted to Bondo, and Chief Elijah OLuoch was replaced with Mr. Samwel Nyawanda who was one of his assistants.

The member of Parliament of Central Nyanza Jaramogi Oginga Odinga condemned the incident in the Legislative Council *Parliament*.In connection with this, councilors Vitalis Asugo, J.M. Assessa with the support of other Central Nyanza African District Council ADC strongly condemned the incident and the then minister for Local Government,Mr. Winfred Havelock dissolved the council because of the Uyoma saga.Before the Madiany meeting the Uyoma elders sent a delegation of Mr. W.W. Adhiambo Wamola and Mr. Ariga wuod Sombe a.k.a Ariga Lot to the then Governor of Kenya Sir. Eveling Baring. The objective of the mission was to consider, the immediate release of their two sons in detention, Mr. Walter Fanuel Odede and Mr. Ramogi Achieng' Oneko. This was on the the grounds that Ramogi Achieng' Oneko had no case to answer according to the trial by Justice Thucker, and Odede was detained without trial.Sir. Dingle Foot, a member for Eaton sent a joint resolution signed by the Chairman of movement for colonial freedom Mr. Fenner Brokeway moved a motion in the House of Commons requesting the British colonial office to release the duo.

Chianda Primary School teacher Mr. Henry Onditti Achola had composed a song with the preamble in praise of the detained Uyoma heroes. The song was sung during the Bondo Zone Choir competition; Mr. Odiwuor and John Ndiewo Apala were the adjudicators.

The song;

Yawa KAU loso piny

Loso piny Loso piny x2

Dak wa parie Achieng' Oneko, wuod Oneko piny thago x2

Dak wa parie Odede Obonyo, wuod Obonyo piny thago x2

Chief Bathlomew Nyabola protested that the song should not be ranked nor be allowed to proceed, but the adjudicators allowed them to proceed.
The Chianda School also presented a traditional song:

Yawa Uyoma onyuolo wuoyi makineno, wuoyi makedo gi sungu

Nonego sungu malich ahinya, ka sungu oneno gigoye bunde

Then the choir master, Mr. Henry Onditti Achola in preamble, said that they wanted to present a song in honour of their son Molo Nyadundo. Chianda was disqualified, Mr Onditi Achola was to be sacked from teaching.The Owila teachers Union under John Martin Asesa and Jacob Dede Bondo took the matter to Nyanza Teachers Union, NATO for further appeal. NATO under Mr. S. G. Ayany took the matter to the High Court and the Court ruled in their favour. The High court ruled that Chianda School should proceed to the National competition.

The Majoni I invasion was nick named 'Majod Mbogo'. Majoni is the Whiteman or the English expression of *Join In*. This sentence or expression was used when the British soldiers were rounding up the men in Uyoma into the Government Police Lorries, ferrying them to Bondo and Kisumu prisons. The expression *"join in* or *join them"* was pronounced by Jo-Uyoma as Joni and the plural is Majoni.

THE 2ND INVASION OF MAJONI IN UYOMA OF 1972

The Uyoma defiance of authority is again witnessed in the second Majoni invasion which erupted from simple sibling wrangles in land dispute. Jo-Uyoma instead of going to the lands office to settle disputed land ownership and beckons, they decided to settle the matter through violence which left several people dropping dead on the ground. The two Kunya families dispute caused disagreement when one family got the service of the Police to help solve the dispute. The other family sort sympathy from the community. During the discusions the unknown police opened fire to save his life and the crowd surged for his life, it is estimated that more than five people lost their lives while several people were injured. The person that I can remember that died was my cousin Ongong'a ,Kochieng' whom we used to call Gagra.

In our home the person whom I clearly remember that was injured was Joshua Midundo Ouya who died 20 years later with two bullets lodged in his body.

When the matter got off hand, the Government called in the Majoni who, this time, caused more havoc than the first Majoni. This time the Majoni were unruly young men and many men were brutally injured to deformity. The women were beaten and raped at the height of independent Kenya.

The invasion was halted when Fanuel Odede appealed for rescue from President Jomo Kenyatta.the invasion of Majoni 2 spread all over Uyoma and very many mistakes were made by the sitting government.

The issue that started off as a simple domestic wrangle turned out to become an issue that spread all over Uyoma because of Jo-Uyoma's historical defiance to authority.

The following story is narrated by Sam Ligongo Ojowa who lives more than ten kilometers from Kunya.

LIGONGO AND LOD MAWIRA

It was 10.00 am in the morning and the little boy Ligongo had just taken the calves and the shoats (sheep and goats) to the grazing field a distance away from the main herd of cattle. It was the time to take the sorghum and millet porridge, but today we were lucky because we had visitors. My mum made chapatti and Dorcas was already sent to buy bread and jam at Manyuanda Shopping Centre.

My father Abisalom Ojowa had many friends and many stories. My favourite topic was *Ojiro Nyamande* (The gallant German soldiers and the *Panyako* (Pioneer Corps) episodes. Today I sat at his knees waiting for the stories. His World War II *Komrado* Aduwo Ibrahim was here with one additional familiar face and two unfamiliar faces. They came with *maliet* or the latest gossip in the season.

Komrado and the story commenced and continued, *Lod Mawira ma Kamolo* (Lord Mayor of Kamolo) has decided to overtake the Lordship of Jo-Nyakinya *Mwalo* to equate himself with Lord Delamere of Nakuru. His name is Ngunya Adhoga and he works with a Company in the Queens Land across the Oceans in Ulaya. He is forcefully evacuating *vinyingarika* from Kayundi across Kunya and into Katweng'a extending to Kogado Wuon Denge. The area mainly covers Joka-Osewe, This clan is the clan that *Jaduk ma Mbogo* (the naked Mbogo) comes from and *Ja-MauMau ma Janeko* (Oneko the MAU MAU leader). The other notable educated Maseno students from Kosewe are Japuonj Dida then Joka-Molo both Ajenge and Ochola. The fact that he works closely with the British and Kenya Government he has managed to subdue Joka-Oneko to the extent that Odede who is very close to Kenyatta has not been able to influence the Government to stop this notorious Lod Mawira. His intention is to build an economic empire that he claims will serve Jo-Uyoma with adequate food supply from horticulture and livestock so that Nyanza does not rely on Rift Valley for essential food commodities.

For me this was the most boring story and I almost slept in the middle of it but the tea was too good. I kept on wondering how big or giantic this Lod Mawira would be, he must be similar to the story of David and Goliath that I was taught last Sunday.

The story rolled back in my mind a week later when we were woken up at 5.00am by the rude soldiers of Lod Mawira, we ran out to see what was happening. I saw men dressed in combat uniforms with buttons and guns and rounding all the men plus my father. This was the first time I saw my father subdued to complete surrender, now I understood Lod Mawira's strength, yes he is a true giant with a big army. When I checked on my mother I did not find her, most of the women had escaped the wrath of Lod Mawira army which I understood later were on rape rampage.

At 10.00 am I was left with no alternative but take the cattle to graze, I instructed my sisters not to release the calves and shoats (sheep and goats) until I came back. After grazing the cattleI I went back home and we opened the door for the calves and the shoat. Before we could take charge all the calves overtook us, heading for their mothers.

By evening we were by ourselves, my two sisters were too young and they could not cook ugali neither could we find the matchbox to light the fire. I went out and milked the few docile cows and we had milk for supper.

That was not an easy day for my father and other villages were surrounded by the Majoni at Pap Kolal. They were kept waiting for the District Commissioner until the late afternoon. When the DO and the DC arrived, they were briefed by the Chief and the Majoni Leader. When the DC stood to address the people, Odingo Majonya stood up and asked the DC why they had been kept in the sun since morning in regard to Kamolo affairs. He said the following. *"Bwana DC ok wan nyithindo ma inyalo keto wa e chieng' ne wach gik mane otimre Kamolo, weche Jo-Kamolo dhi itiek gi Jok-Amolo."* Poor Odingo Majonya was thrown into the waiting Police lorry and all the rest of the men voluntarily jumped in the packed Lorries and they were driven to Bondo Police Station on several trips. The women who were kept on the otherside of the field fled back to their homes.

My father and many of the men were set free except the notorious men led by Odingo Majonya,

When I started work in Nairobi I was very fortunate to meet the man Ngunya Andhoga, I changed my mind about him. I met a soft spoken Gentleman of first class order. The stories I had near my father were truly *Maliet*.

THE REMOVAL OF THE DISTRICT HEADQUARTERS IN 2012

Rarieda was made a District in 2007 by the Kibaki's administration during the tenure of Honourable Raphael Tuju as the Rarieda constituency member of Parliament.

A District Commissioner was posted to Rarieda without a definite administration office. Upon hearing of the posting of the commissioner, the two communities; Asembo and Uyoma started lobbying for the citing of the District headquater in their respective divisional headquarters.

The Uyoma people were mobilized under the leadership of Nelson Oreng' Juma, Jack Owenda, Mrs. Monica Olali, amongst many others.

A meeting for both communities, Uyoma and Asembo was called by the District Commissioner Mr. Kinyua at Gagra Primary School. The following noted personalities were in attendance and addressed the gathering; The former District Commissioner Mr. Calisto Akello, Peter Aete Samba, Washington Appollo Juma, a Representative of Luo Council of elders - Jack Nguono Hongo, Akello Gwela and Hon Nicholas Odero Gumbo attended as the then sitting MP. The meeting reached a deadlock and each side was asked to select six people to form a District citing committee which was to be chaired by the District Commisioner, who was considered to be neutral in the process. The six people who represented Uyoma were; Mr. Nelson Oreng' Juma, Jack Owenda, Mornica Olali, Dalmas Orwa Midega, Dr. Joseph Okweso and Dr. Ambrose Misore.

The Uyoma elites were mobilized. They contributed financial and material support towards harmonization of the citing of the District headquarters wherever it was to be agreed.

The District headquater was later re-located to Asembo at Rarieda boardering Uyoma. Jo-Uyoma were not pleased by the movement of the headquarters. One day it is believed that Uyoma will be autonomous.

.KEY LESSONS LEARNT FROM TURMOILS

So it came to pass that the sitting government blew the majoni 2 saga out of proportion and Jo-Uyoma young men here called gladiators knew that they were the major targets of the sitting government forces.

Based on historical turmoilss starting from the attacks in Kawango, Gunda Uyoma in Alego Kobare, the Sakwa distraction on arrival from Kawango, the hostility in Kanyamwa, the Mumbo massacre, the British government invasion of Mumbo Massacre, to add salt to the wound, the british recorded the hostility led by Jonathan Okwiri followed by Odede Obonyo and then the coming of Mau Mau of Achieng' Oneko crowned by the thurgish behavior of Oruko Makasembo and Mbogo Mandera and his followers, the Uyoma men knew that the government of the day will slaughtger them the way they killed gladiators in the Mumbo massacre where many young warriors were slaughtered.

The gladiators included the following; Molo Nyadundo, Otieno Osogo, Ongoro Nyapende, Ogutu Anyieche, Nange Oluga, Onoka Maugo, Omondo Adhura among others.

In majoni 1,the memory dawned on Jo-Uyoma that several young men reffered to as gladiators were injured and maimed, they were led by Mbogo Mandera,others that were injured include the following, Abonyo Oyombe, Otuoma Abila, Omil Kokokola, Ochido Macharia, Mariko Odipo, Anyumba Nyamor, Were Apete, Osimba Milewa,Orako Wuon Agire, Ogola Wuon Walala and Kere Wuon Odhil among others.

The Uyoma gladiators knew very well that Majoni were coming specifically for them because of their notorious history and developed a specific strategic plan to ensure that the government was going to loose in this battle.

The first step was *Yore Yore Yore* the whole of Uyoma to alert every young man that the enemy was coming. They then blew the horn (*tung'*) which is one of the major signals of war alertness.

The word was sent out that every young man would go and get a hallow papyrus reed which would help in breathing under water.

It was agreed that all the gladiators from Kamariga, Obenge, Likungu,Bar -Kogonga, Osindo ,Misori, Nyangoye, Luanda –Kotieno, Kamin Oningo, Nyamanga, Wi-kwang', Madundu, Mayange, Gudwa, Kopiata, Kasiri, Lela, Kunya, Adola, Kogonga, Kaswara, Ndiru, Kayundi, Ukunja, Oyawore, and, Aram were to ready themselves to distract the government forces (Majoni) to run after them as they shouted *yore, yore, yore,*. It is interesting to note that when they ~~illulated~~ ululated *yore yore, yore,* the government forces foolishly followed the sound in every beach to attack and they corked their guns and unleashed their dogs. At this point in every beach, the gladiators slowly swimming backwardly dropped into the known waters with their hollow reeds in their mouths and noses to assist them breath under water. They waited and beckoned the government forces to follow them with their guns and dogs and they quickly dived into the water.

It is not a miracle that Uyoma gladiators were superstar swimmers, this was evident in Kawango during the drowning of Kawango children into river Wuoroya (*Lisimu*) every Uyoma child from the age of five is trained on how to swim. The guns were obsolete and of no use to the officers as there was nobody to shoot; the trained police dogs were then unleashed towards the gladiators. The game was as such, the young men would protrude their heads above the water, and when the dogs saw, they lashed out into the waters, as the dogs came, the gladiators went under the water and one by one they pulled and drawned the police dogs into the water, the dogs succumbed to the heavy waters of lake Victoria and died.

More than 20% of the police dogs that were brought into Uyoma died in the beaches of Uyoma but the Uyoma gladiators survived.

The real culprits of majoni 2 led by Osewe Ojode, known as Njang' Njing' Njong' and Ogare Aduodo Okew Joka Olualo from Kunya Kosewe *nind gilepi* (sleep alert) led the historical marathon swim of 8 hours across the Lake from Kunya in Siaya county to Huma hills in Homabay county.

THE LAKE TRAGEDY OF 1985

The youths from Uyoma especially from great Rageng'ni sub-location formed one football club under the coach and captainship of Onyango Nyiera a.k.a Onyango Wuod Ayoma who had lived in both Nairobi and Mombasa for some years and had a lot of soccer knowledge.

It was during the august holidays and after the bumper crops harvest that the fifteen Uyoma youths made a football tournament appointment with their counterparts in 'Norway' South Nyanza. Most of the youths were siblings from the same family like the sons of Ajenge from Kunya.

The match was to start at 3.00 p.m. The boys had organized to travel in the boat of Mzee Ajenge whose two sons were also members of the team. The Kunya group boarded the boat and roared to Kogonga beach to collect both boys from Kayundi and Kogonga areas. They started their journey for Norway South Nyanza at 2.00p.m. The boys were very hopeful and were to travel back the next day, which never was.

Amid the journey, a very heavy wind started blowing, there was storm. The colour of the lake changed from blue to dark green and a thick cloud formed in the atmosphere. A sign of danger. They tried to row but it was unfortunate, the wind was too much, and the worse came to pass. Their cry to a business man who was rowing comfortably with his goats to the opposite direction fell on deaf ears. He argued that if he tried to help them, he would lose his goats and business. The boat was hit by the storm and it capsized.

Only one person survived the accident by clinging on the part of the boat. Some families lost more than one member in the tragedy and painful enough the dead boys were from the same village. An eerie of sadness filled the area for a whole year.

Uyoma men and women were mobilized from all over the country through the efforts of Lwande Oneko to assist in the burial preparations.

The then councilor, Henry Ouma Okendo assisted by incurring the expense of buying the coffins for the dead.

The lake took away the lives of young Uyoma men in their quest to popularize their land through sports.

WHEN THE HUNTER BECOMES THE HUNTED

Uyoma as a peninsular enjoys the use of lake waters both for commercial and domestic purposes. There are several beaches stretching from Aram the boarder of Uyoma and Asembo to Kamariga our boarder with Sakwa people.

There are several winds which control the movement of the lake. The lake is not flat as some may think.

Apart from fish. The lake is inhabited by both dangerous reptiles and animals like crocodiles and hippos.

The hippos are very disastrous especially to the farmers, they feast and triumph on the crops and vegetables. This is rampant during the rainy season of the month of March to July.

The crocodiles attack and feast on both animals and human beings especially those which stray into their territories.

Several reports have been heard and read over the media of how these gigantic terror reptiles and animals have become a terror to human beings.

During the late forties and early fifties there was a man from Kosewe clan along Kunya beach who specialized in the hunting and trapping of crocodiles using traditional traps.

The man became so wealthy from the crocodile skins and parts business. It is interesting that this man had made a watch tower while fishing so as to have a good view of the crocodiles and enable him trap them.

One fateful day, after the hunter had finished his fishing business and decided to descend from the tower having checked and verified that the reptiles were not around and that he was safe to descend, this day the reptile was more watchful and decided to hide under the shadow of the tower ready to attack at the slightest opportunity.

While the hunter was trying to descend from the tower, the crocodile followed from behind and descended on him, catching him on the leg. Being a brave hunter, He struggled with the crocodile and managed to get out of the water but without his left leg which was broken and swallowed by the crocodile.

CULTURAL CHARACTERISTICS OF JO-UYOMA

Before we discuss the Uyoma characteristics, it is important to document a simple profile of Uyoma and some interesting issues or stories.

Uyoma comprises of sloppy land scape towards Lake Victoria, thus confirming the area as a lakeside country.

The soils are predominantly black cotton soils, suitably utilized for the cultivation of Maize, Millet, Beans, peas, Groundnuts, cotton, sunflower and with high potential of horticultural production.

The area experiences modified equatorial climate with temperatures ranging between 27^0C to 36^0C .During the months of December to mid – March, the area is dry .The rains are predominantly widespread between Mid –March, April and May. The major source of income in the area includes subsistence farming, horticultural production and small scale trading involving cereals, livestock and fishing.

Uyoma is the only area in Nyanza where people can plant without fertilizers and realize a bamper harvest, it is known for high yields of Millet, Maize, Beans, Groundnuts, Cowpeas pumpkins and other horticultural products such as Tomato, Water Mellon among others.

Uyoma has some "don'ts and dos" and beliefs, they are as follows:

During planting season mature girls or married women who were born in Uyoma known as *Wagog'ni* were not allowed to visit their parents because they would be used as sacrificial lambs to induce rainfall for bamper harvest.

In Uyoma, strangers were not allowed to praise the bamper harvest or speak or marvel at the crops in the farm because the crops would 'speak' to them. This was regarded as very bad omen and a curse, infact one could easily become deaf or dumb.

In Uyoma mushrooms could also echo their opinion and speak to strangers or those who return home during the harvesting season. The mushrooms would request to find out where one had been hiding during the ploughing, planting and weeding seasons only to reappear during harvest. This is known in Luo as *Oyundi wadhi puodho- aol, oyundi wadhi doyo- atuo*. While at the harvesting time, it is *Oyundi nise se se*.

Red-billed firefinch (male)- (Oyundi)

In Uyoma Children were warned not to laugh at a donkey when farting or polluting the air otherwise your mouth would crack. *Nyithindo ne ok oyienegi Nyiero Ka punda yuak to Kuodho nikech dhogi ne biro barore.*

Children were strictly warned never to kill *Ochinjo*

otherwise their mothers houses would be engulfed with fire and burn down to ashes.

 Children were warned never to kill frogs- *ogwal*, because if you killed a frog your mother's breast would drop.

Thieves and bandits were warned never to try and raid livestock from Uyoma because the Owila magic would make them loose memory and direction and their compasses would direct them towards the lake shores instead of the escape route which passed Aram.

Once a woman had been married in Uyoma and dowry had been paid she could not desert her marital home. If she tried to escape she would lose direction and instead she would find herself in another Uyoma homestead before reaching the boundary of Uyoma at the entry of Asembo or Sakwa.

All these teachings and issues had their positive rationale and they emanate from the Luo and Uyoma history, traditions, cultural issues and even environmental conservation. The historical factors include draught and famine which are natural calamities brought about by geographical and climatic conditions, they can be summoned as environmental factors.

The turmoils that Jo-Uyoma have faced through history have shaped their character tradition and wellbeing. Many people view Jo-Uyoma as brave, fierce, violent with warrior like characteristic, others view them as intricate and believers of magic and traditional medicine men *Jogo mohero bilo kod ndagla*. When we look at bravery, it is possible to conclude that they are brave when you consider the Kanyamwa wars by the Uyoma gladiators seen as hired marcenaries, the confrontation of the very armed and organized British Soldiers at the Mumbo Massacre or the exhibited courage of Odede that enabled him to take over Chairmanship of KAU from Kenyatta at the height of Mau Mau emergency of 1952.

The following are some of the fears that many people have about Uyoma:

Before we delve into some of these cultural issues, it is important to clarify the understanding of culture and the issues that have led Jo-Uyoma to behave in a certain manner and then form some unique characteristics. According to the English dictionary, culture is described as "a way of life". It is the arts, customs and habits that characterize a particular society or nation. It involves the beliefs, values, behavior and material objects that constitute a people's way of life.This way of life is moulded by environmental factors, these environmental factors include Geographical, Religious, Economic, Socio-cultural, political or historical events and Scientific factors amomg others.

The Geographical factors include the terrain, vegetation and weather conditions among others. The major geographical factor that has affected Jo-Uyoma is the locational position; it is located at the extreme end of the southern part of Siaya County right into the Lake Victoria and surrounded by Lake except the narrow entrance through Aram at Migwa on one side and Got Abiero at the other end. This site meant that there were very few visitors because the other neighbours could only access the Uyoma through the Lake, this made Jo-Uyoma secluded. The second issue is that thieves such as cattle rustlers could not easily enter Uyoma without being noticed during the day. It was common for all visitors to be interviewed and worse interrogated as they travelled into Uyoma, Jo-Uyoma were always suspiciuos about strangers.The other reason was that there was nowhere else one would be travelling to because Uyoma is surrounded by the Lake and it is the last and extreme part of Siaya County.Members of the Uyoma community knew one another and practiced community policing, it was logical to ask the visitor the home of destination. Uyoma is surrounded by the mass of Lake Victoria waters which made it difficult for the thieves to leave the place at night because of water reflections which are like motorvehicle flood lights. It is also interesting to note that during dark seasons, at night Uyoma is as dark as black and you cannot see anything five metres away. In the history of Uyoma all cattle thieves were found circulating within Uyoma by early morning and they would abandon their project.One of the Mama Na Dada volunteers called Sue Bell commented that she had been to several places in Kenya but there is nowhere that the night is as dark as Uyoma Kunya. During my youth when we went for night dances or discos in Uyoma we had to have among us a person who knew the Uyoma terrain such as Wire Omolo or Oyaro Odhach otherwise losing direction and then getting lost was very easy with the massive trees and bushes. Uyoma was and has been virgin land; it is of the very few locations where crops or staple food like maize and millet are planted once a year. The farm produce in Uyoma has been remarkable because the use of fertilizer and manure is unknown and the yield per acre was very high, and size of the plants was scarery *ababari*. During the harvesting season no visitors were entertained in Uyoma. The harvest was then stored in granaries and it is always enough to feed families until the next annual harvest and beyond. Uyoma was known as the land of plenty. Livestock was in plenty and milk abundant plus overflowing fish supply. The farming and fishing made Jo-Uyoma egoistic and self conceited. Uyoma created an elite society that was self sufficient as such Uyoma remained a closed society that could easily remain in the past ages. Uyoma hardly needed assistance from outside. In Uyoma oxen ploughs, produce such as ground nuts would be left in the fields and nobody would touch or steal them because of these magical beliefs. It can be recorded that even as we write this book, livestock are still left outside in the open. If by any chance or mistake one lays their hands on these Uyoma properties you will sure be killed.

THIEVES DO NOT THRIVE IN UYOMA

Recently in January 2015, the Secretary for Internal Security Hon. Joseph Nkaissery said 'Security begins with you". This means that security is best handled by the Community, therefore Community policing is the foundation of security in the community. *Miji Kumi* (the ten homes) has been very successful in Tanzania in regard to Community Management and Policing. Uyoma has informally practiced Community policing that even the greatest Livestock Raider - Migele from Seme avoided Uyoma. Migele (Ja- Kochomo)-a nickname he got from his ability to deform the horns of cattle so as to confuse the owners) was known as a consultant and practitioner in the Livestock Raiding. Migele has the legacy of plastic surgery of cows, he would transplant the horns and even the owner of the cow could not recognize his cow.

A few Community Policing incidences have been documented from Uyoma.

CATTLE RUSTLING IN UYOMA IS BUT A HUSTLE

A renowned cattle rustler, Migele from Seme said "Go and carryout cattle rustling in Luo lands but do not attempt Uyoma" (*Kwel uru e dho udi duto ma ei Luo to kik utem Uyoma*)

The Luo community has close blood relation with other communities such as the Kalenjins and Maasai and they both kept large herds of cattle. The Luo, Maasai and the Kalenjin were known to practice cattle rustling. Their young men would go out to raid cattle from their neighbours as a show of bravery and also to accumulate wealth. Livestock especially cattle among many African Community was a sign of wealth, leadership and a person with large herds of cattle commandend respect in the community. Cattle were and are still being used to pay dowry, were used during batter trade, milk and meat from the cattle are used as food, skin from cattle make good leather, horns from cows make musical instruments. Owila trained Uyoma Gladiators to raid their neighbours while they lived in Alego Kobare. The practice was perfected and helped them survive the hostile Kanyamwa hostility.

NG'IELA NO NG'IEL

There lived a group of cattle rustlers from Luo community like Mbije Kodero and Miruka who hailed from Uyoma, Ngi'ela and Ogolla son of Opedhi both from Sakwa and their leader Migele Ja- Kadero Nduru in the land of Seme. Together, they would lead young men to raid cattle from the neighbouring villages and Locations.

In 1974, Mbije being a local boy from Uyoma was asked by his group members to arrange so that they could steal from the villages in Uyoma, they then consulted Migele ja-Kadero Nduru (Ja-Kochomo) whose expertise and advice would be handy at such times. Until now people from Seme are reffered to as Jo-Kochomo. Migele having known the history of Uyoma was not comfortable and he therefore advised them against raiding Uyoma for it was known not to be friendly with such vices and anybody who tried would not survive to tell the story.

Ng'iela did not heed Migele's advice and went ahead with Mbije and Ogolla to raid Mzee Oballa's home in Kakremba-Kogonga village in Uyoma Kabudha.

They arrived at the homestead at 2.00 am in the deep night and went ahead to the pen which was at the centre of the homestead according to the Luo tradition. When the dogs noticed strange people in the cattle pen, they started barking to alert the people but when Mzee Oballa looked through the window and saw people in the pen untying cattle and goading them away, he went back to his house without raising an alarm and waited for the raiders to leave his compound. That was when he did what the Uyoma people do best. He came out of his hut with a traditional stool and placed it next to the entrance of the pen and started shouting *Yore! Yore! Yore!* (Block the paths x3). The *Yore Yore* chant echoed to Rageng'ni, to Gagra into Kobong' and Ko-Kwiri and Uyoma woke up, they came out with spears, pangas and rungus, blocking all the paths leading away from the village.

By this time the raiders were moving towards Simenya River, and when they herd the war songs around the village, fear gripped them and they scattered in different directions, mbije being a local, found his way to his home, leaving the cattle in the field known as Pap-Matera, the villagers having surounded the village, started throwing spears all over and Ng'iela was hit on his leg. But as the saying goes, thieves die hard. He managed to run with the bleeding leg upto the road leading to Kisumu where he was lucky to get a Kisumu bound bus – which he boarded at Yawo Kosewe. Uyoma people having known the tricks of the thieves sent some of their men like Ogallo wuon Ooro to Aram market, lest the thieves escaped through that route. When the bus arrived at Aram, the men who were on the watch stopped it and asked if there was any suspicious person in the vehicle, for they were tracking some cattle rusttlers and the driver having been born and brought up in Uyoma told them that a strange man had boarded the bus between Rageng'ni and Aram, Ng'iela had by that time realized why Migele - the consultant did not give his blessing on the raid on Uyoma land, the passengers noticed his strange behavior and pushed him out of the vehicle.

The men tied Ng'iela and dragged him up to Pap-Matera where they had left the animals. This is when the villagers realized that he was a stranger and asked him to tell them the person who had directed him to the village for it is common knowledge that a stranger does not raid a village unless he is assisted by insiders. When he insisted that he was alone, He was asked to lie down, and they chopped off both his limbs placing them on his side. The pain prompted Ng'iela to name the Mbije as the person who had brought him to that village and that Mbije disappeared when they were cornered.

Mbije who was known by the villagers for his cunning ways was then tracked to his home where he was found pretending to be in a deep sleep. He was equally dragged to Pap-Matera next to Ng'iela where they were both hacked to death by the villagers.

And so the saying goes that *Ng'iela ne ong'iel gi Uyoma,* Ng'iela was floored by Uyoma

Up to this day, there is a dirge among the Uyoma people which goes- ("*Adola lich ok wuothie nono makata okumba makata tong*") Adola is dengarous; you must walk around with a spear and a shield.

ORONDI OKWEMBA

A young man named Orondi Okwemba who was brought up in his maternal grand parents' home in Uyoma among the Wagoro clan. He was recruited by Cattle thieves from Alego and Sakwa in the belief that having known the ways of Jo-Uyoma, he would be their point man in their attempt to steal livestock in Uyoma.

Orondi, with the assistance of his friends went to the cattle shed of one of his uncles at about 10.00 p.m and stole a fattened bull which would fetch a lot of money in the market. As usual Ogaja, Orondi's uncle woke up at 3.00 a.m to inspect his home as thieves were known to strike at around this time. He started with the cattle shed and to his surprise, Openda - the fattened bull was missing. Being the month of April when crops were in the fields and having suspected that the bull might have broken the tether, he woke up his nephew to help him look for the bull lest it destroy the neighbours' crops.

This time, the clever Orondi, who was pretending to be in deep sleep had gone with the bull all the way from Wagoro to Wichlum beaches where with the assistance of his friends, he went into the middle of the papyrus reeds and tied the bull, waiting for a market day when it would be easy for him to join the trail of other cattle traders on their way to Bondo market, where he would meet his friends who would then transfer it to Gem or Alego. He then returned home just before 1.00 a.m, and went to bed.

Orondi woke up, and after getting the report of the missing bull from his uncle, he started alerting neighbours with the *yore yore* alarm, ignoring his uncle's suggestion that they go out to the nearby farms to look for the bull.

The neighbours came out in numbers, blocked the paths leading to Aram, Owimbi, Madiany and Amoyo. They searched till morning but there was no trace of the bull, the young men came back dejected, but were sure that the bull was still within the borders of Uyoma, Asembo and Sakwa. But as the saying goes, "*Jakuo makwali ema konyi menyo mondo omed lali*" Orondi advised his uncle that he was sure, the thieves must had taken the Asembo route along the shores of Lake Victoria, or, even crossed over to Karachuonyo through Kunya or Mbita through Luanda Kotieno. He was totally against the search going to Sakwa. All this time, nobody suspected him, save for a few mischievous youths who scolded him for having slept like a woman when the thieves were raiding his uncles home,only to raise an alarm when they were long gone, others jockingly asked if he had been bribed by the thieves. He himself participated actively in the daily search, always leading people away from Sakwa.

Word having gone around all the villages of Uyoma and the neighbouring Asembo and Sakwa, every body kept an eye. On the third day, Tuesday, being the market day at the famous Bondo livestock market, Orondi woke up earlier than usual and hastily left home. His uncle assumed that he had gone for the search, but Orondi had gone to Wichlum beach where he had hidden the bull so that he could take it to Bondo market. It was easier to lead the bull to Bondo on a market day since many traders would be on their way with herds of cattle and so it would not raise any suspicion.This was also the day that the cattle traders of Uyoma were prepared to trace their kin's stolen bull for they were very sure, from their experience, that the bull was still in Uyoma or its environs.

The first traders who arrived in the market informed the market council and leaders that *Ruath Rapenda* had been stolen from Uyoma two days ago, and their instinct told them that the thief might bring it to the market, either for sale or onward transportation. The market elders, then, gave instruction to all traders that they should not buy or sell any livetock outside the market fences, and as was their custom, all the traders, would go by the words of their leaders.

Orondi's colleagues who had also arrived in the market and were trying to trace him became suspicious of the announcement and took off, for the bull that the elders were describing, was the same one they had come to pick.

When Orondi approached the place where they had agreed to meet his friends, he could not see them, after along wait, he called a young boy and sent him to the stock market to call any trader who wanted to buy a bull, The boy asked where the bull was since his father was a trader and would be willing to buy, but he insisted that the boy call the trader from the market first. When the boy reached the stock market, he heard the traders being worned against buying or selling outside the stock market boundaries, he tried to trace his father but could not see him, so he went to the markert leader and told him of a man who had sent him to call for him a buyer for his bull. The elders instantly, knew that indeed, this was the bull they were trying to trace. He then called a few traders, including Ong'ala Mbe from Uyoma and after he had whispered to them, Ong'ala asked the boy to lead him to the man.

The other four men followed at a distance, and waited until the young boy and Ong'ala had started negotiating with Orondi. Meanwhile the bull was hidden in a small thicket across the road, as they moved towards the bull, the other men joined and as they concluded the price negotiation and ready to shake hands as a sign of agreement, Ong'ala held Orondi's hand tightly and shouted *yore ,yore,yore!* Within seconds, the place was surrounded. And Orondi could not escape; his day for reckoning had come.

When traders from Uyoma realized that their kin's bull had been recoverd and the suspected thief was their nephew, they insisted that the bull and the thief be taken back to the scene of crime which was in Uyoma. Orondi having known how thieves were dealt with in Uyoma begged to be left with the police at Bondo for he feared the wrath of Jo-Uyoma but both the police and the market elders agreed to let Jo-Uyoma take their bull and nephew back to the scene of crime, meanwhile word had reached Uyoma that Ogaja's bull was actually stolen by his nephew Orondi, and he had been caught in Bondo trying to sell it. The youth set off to Bondo baying for Orondi's blood and they met the traders from Bondo with the bull and Orondi at Amoyo market on their way from Bondo. Amoyo is in the border between Sakwa and Uyoma Kagwa.

The young men first of all insisted that Orondi explain how he was able to escape with the bull. He offered to explain thinking that his uncles would spare him, he even pleaded that he was *Nyathi-migigo* and so they could have mercy on him.

When he finished explaining, Ongong'a, who led the three day search for the bull announced, 'to serve as a lesson to all those who were planning to raid Uyoma, this is his punishment… he tied a rope around the bulls neck, then tied it around Orondi''s waist having also tied his legs and hands, he then led the bull, dragging Orondi from Amoyo to Wagoro, his flesh dropping and blood oozing from his mouth, nose and ears.Orondi died just before reaching the chief's camp being dragged by the bull he had stollen.

OWUODHO NGONONGONO

In Uyoma Kabudha around Rageng'ni village, young tall dark skinned and handsome man who was born and brought up in Uyoma suddenly turned into a rapist, he nick named himself *Ngonongono*.

This rape episode went on and was so bad that women would not dare leave their homes either late in the evening or very early in the morning. The young girls would only leave their homes for school in the morning under the escort of their fathers or elder brothers and only when the fathers or brothers were strong enough to wrestle Ngonongono. Women who traded in the market or beaches would have to walk in groups so as to avoid being raped.

When all the young women and girls decided to either walk in groups or in the company of men who would protect them from this cruel young man, he changed his game and decided to prey on very old and lonely women who were widowed and had no one to protect them. Owuodho would break into their houses and rape them repeatedly and because of the stigma associated with rape, most of these old women suffered silently as the young rascal celebrated.

When it was finally known that he was a rapist, he shifted the torment to old women.. He would get into these houses during the day when the old women were busy in the gardens, hide himself under the bed, wait for the woman to finish all her chores and as soon as the woman retired to bed, he would gag them and carry them on his shoulders into the thickets where he would finally rape them as he wished.

One day, young boys who had gone to look after their cattle and decided to play hide and seek in the bushes, they came across an old lady whom they knew very well, lying helplessly in the bush with her mouth gagged, they rushed to the nearby homestead and alerted them. They moved swiftly and took the woman to the hospital where she later narrated the story to the well wishers. The woman did not want it to be known that she had been raped and therefore refused to report the incident to the police.

The villagers then took the initiative to curb the vice. Men would stroll around the village the whole night, checking on the old women and young widows. Others offering to keep vigil around such homes in groups armed with rungus. The serial rapist, having realized that his days were numbered, decided to steal his parent's cattle and cross over to Homabay County. The boat owners refused to carry the cattle to Homa Bay. He left the cattle along the shores of Lake Victoria- Kunya beach and disappeared.

In his notorious episodes he broke the arm of a Policeman. Later a girl from Okela Secondary School died after being raped. The Uyoma terrorist was on the rampage. The Police were finding it difficult to tame this man. The Chiefs could not contain him either. Community policing and vigilante was launched. Now the hunting of the notorious Owuodho was set in motion. The Uyoma gladiators armed themselves and started hunting for the terrorist.

He moved to hide in Lela Kasiri; the hunters smoked him out of the bushes. He moved to Kunya Beach where he met the wrath of the fishermen but they could not face him because he was armed to the teeth. All they could do is to shout *Yore Yore Yore*. The shouting alerted the hunters who moved swiftly to Kunya Beach. Owuodho was swift and disappeared to Wadh Omena and then to Kayundi towards Nyamasore. *Yore Yore Yore* alerted the Kayundi community and roads were blocked. Owuodho was now sandwiched and a rain of stones met him from both sides. The Police force from Aram was alerted. By the time the Police arrived Owuodho was overwhelmed and on the ground. The community defied the Police and they stoned Owuodho to death. His body was still warm when it was loaded in the Police Van. This is not mob justice, this is community policing.

MOULDING OF THE UNIQUE CHARACTER OF UYOMA

Now let us look at events and upheavals that faced Jo-Uyoma along their historical path that has moulded the unique characteristics. The depature from Kawango was a classic picture of arrogance coated with-pride that caused long enemity between Kawango and Jo-Uyoma. This part of history created the urge for Jo-Uyoma to develop the love for ancestral land at the burial site of the Uyoma patriarch the great Omia Ramul at Thurmony. Owila pointed to Got Naya as the landmark for Jo-Uyoma and Got Naya has remained the most significant spot and the heart beat of Uyoma. All religious ceremonies and traditional rituals have been carried out at this point. The rituals have been carried prior to battles; prayers have been conducted in the face of draught, famine and other calamities. It is believed that there are many traditional magics that have been performed on Got Naya. Even though Owila's grave stone was buried at Thurmony, many people believe it is pitched at the peak of Got Naya. It is also known that some unscrupulous people have been scavaging and prospecting Got Naya for Uyoma historical ornaments. For example some people went to Got Naya in search for the magical pot that was used during the return from Kanyamwa.

Thurmony, today known as Madiany remains the central point and headquarters of Uyoma and all formal, official and informal rituals and ceremonies are conducted at this point. During the departure to

Kanyamwa the blind Midega Ralong'o wept in the boat while from Uyoma and instructed his offsprings to ensure they returned to the ancestral land and told them, "Make sure you multiply, regroup and recapture Got Naya that is your ancestral land." In Kanyamwa Uyoma warriors and gladiators trained themselves to become excellent war marcenaries and they won every battle while supporting their Kanyamwa kins men, Omia Ramul is the Uyoma patriarch while his brother Chwanya is the Kanyamwa patriarch. The Uyoma military supremacy propelled Uyoma gladiators to admiration and hatred among the neighbours and they had to leave Kanyamwa unceremoniously, they were ready to recapture the ancestral land based on their war skills and modern weapons. This arrogance -and war like behavior drove Jo-Uyoma to defy the British military and plunged them into the Mumbo Massacre that led to untold misery and great loss of lives and property. The Mumbo Masscre built permanent hatred towards the British, its rule and his introduction to Christianity.

The resistance led to poor education growth with minimal Colonial Government support for other amenities. The Anglican Church in Ranalo is 10 miles from Kunya but three women trekked every Sunday for prayers and these were Dorca Pande (Mrs. Dorca Oyaro Oneko) Odinga Nya Nyandawa (Mrs Christabel Odande) and Okuku Nyo Owino (Mrs. Jedida Achieng Oneko). As a child, I used to follow these three women to Ranalo. They would only realize that I was following them at the church entrance a point I was very sure they could not chase me to go back home. My objective was to meet Jesus, I knew that he lives in Maseno but could possibly visit us in Ranalo on a Sunday, since he was the son of God, and Ranalo was God's house. I waited from 1950s to date for him to come to his Ranalo *kanisa* invain.

During my youthful days, Maseno was the only school that students were referred to from sector (basic) schools.

All the schools were started by the missionaries and one of the conditions for the students to join the school was baptism and acquiring a foreign name; Okwiri ka Nyakinya was baptized to Jonathan Okwiri, Arina Oulo to Richard Arina, Odede to Walter Fanuel Odede, Achieng Oneko to Richard Achieng Oneko, Oginga Odinga to Adonija Oginga Odinga. Later, most of the individuals abandoned their foreign names and acquired Luo indigenious names like Richard Achieng Oneko to Ramogi Achieng Oneko, Adonija Oginga Odinga to Jaramogi Oginga Odinga, Rosemary Akinyi Mboya to Alaki Akinyi Mboya, Benard Ooko Ombaka to Oki Ooko Ombaka. My name Michael, is only in my Identity card and so my name remains Lwande Oneko

If you come from Uyoma, did you realize that because of the hostility to visitors there are no foreign investors in Uyoma? The most adventurous Asian Dukawallas never had a shop in Uyoma and the nearest was in Kamito in Asembo, there are no Europeans Church leaders that have lived in Uyoma until yesterday. Even after independence and the recent past there are no Kikuyu entrepreneurs or Somalis with their Garrisa shops in Uyoma. People from other tribes that run businesses in Uyoma have some relationship through marriage and other assimilado relationships. The most entrepreneurial people in the World are usually foreigners, if there are no investors in Uyoma then economic growth can be difficult to realize.

The recentment of visitors or foreigners was promoted by the rampant slave trade through Lake Victoria to Uganda, the forceful recruitment into World War I and World War II. The British domination through colonization with taxes, forceful administration, poor governance with discrimination of the African as a third class citizen in his own Country

The hostility of Uyoma to the visitors and neighbours has through time created unity of belongingness among Jo-Uyoma, all people in Uyoma refer to each other as relatives and references are brother, son, father, daughter, sister, mother and in-law and other Luos gape and this Jo-Uyoma reference.

Let us now look at the leaders, heroes and gladiators that have shaped and moulded the history of Uyoma, Siaya and Kenya at large

THE LEADERS, HEROES AND THE GLADIATORS OF UYOMA

The leaders, Heroes and Gladiators are case studies of people with exemplary achievements and have contributed immensly to the wellbeing of the people of Uyoma. The chapter is basically a documentation of Uyoma a few selected Heroes and Gladiators.

DILANG' WUOD ODHIRIANY

Dilang' is the first son of Odhiriany while Owila is the second son. Dilang' led Jo-Uyoma to Kawango and he remained the patriarch of Jo-Uyoma until his death in Kawango. He was a man who had very good rapport and he made friends with Jo-Kawango, Jo-Ugenya and the neighbouring Kalenjin. He learnt bow and arrow fighting skills from the Kalenjin; he knew the Kalenjin military strategies and livestock rustling especially the night raiding. He was a keen military trainer for self defence; he spent his time training his kinsmen while grazing and at leisure time.

OWILA WUOD ODHIRIANY

Owila was the second born son of Odhiriany, he is not the immediate follower of Dilang', there are about three or four sisters between Owila and Dilang'. Owila was very young when Jo-Uyoma moved from the present Uyoma to Kawango. He got married while on transit to Kawango. He was a keen military student of his elder brother Dilang' who a very skillful trainer. Owila admired his brothers military and leadership skills. When Dilang' died he took over the leadership of Jo-Uyoma.

Owila was a very different character from his brother, he pursued economic ambition unlike his brother Dilang', they were like the biblical Jacob and Esau respectively. He wanted to be wealthy, so he made his people to become great famers and he extended his land ownership. This land extension was not welcomed by Jo-Kawango but they tolerated him. Slowly and carefully he led night cattle raidings among his neighbours and when this was discovered by Jo-Kawango their relationship started to erode. Owila was basically a very rough person who encouraged his young boys to frustrate the neighbour's children, the worst culprit was his own son Omolo Ng'ong'o. Owila had very little respect for his relatives but he guided and protected his family jealously.

When his son Omolo Ng'ong'o and his siblings bullied the other children, he always encouraged them. When Jo-Kawango called meetings to discuss the bulling and the bad behaviour of Uyoma children, Owila completely ignored them.

Owila's dream was that, one day he would return to his ancestral land in the present Uyoma where his father Odhiriany and his grandfather Omia Ramul were buried. Based on his dream and poor relationship with Jo-Kawango he led his people from Kawango and temporarily settled in Alego Kobare at the present Gunda Uyoma. When he settled at Alego Kobare he unleashed terror on his neighbours, he even raided his own cousin Matar.

Owila instructed his people to return to Uyoma and he showed them Got Naya while on top of Got Mwer or Ng'iya in Alego. Owila died and was buried in Gunda Uyoma, but his grave stone was carried to Uyoma and symbolically buried at Madiany.

Owila is recognized as the Uyoma patriarch, this is because he out shines his brother Dilang' who was polite.

OMOLO NG'ONGO

Omolo Ngo'ngo' was born in Kawango and his name is Omolo, he was the eldest son of Owila, but the word Ngo'ngo' is a Baluhya poor propnounciation of the Luo word *Ng'ongo* which means elder or senior. The seniors in families are usually given preference and hence the reference of Omolo Ng'ongo.

Omolo remains in the Uyoma history as the one who made the creation of the word Uyoma. Jo-Kawango spoke and even today they speak a cocktail of Bantu dialect mixed with very many Luo words. The Bantu influence in their language makes difficult to pronounce Luo words correctly. The word Uyoma is yet again a Baluhya poor pronounciation of the word *oyuma*. When Omolos' bad childish games brought injuries and finally the death of a Kawango boy, Jo-Kawango called for several meetings but these meetings were dismissed by Jo-Uyoma as childish games or jokes known in Luo as *oyuma*. Jo-Kawango used to refer to them as *Joyuma*, which means jokers. This reference of jokers in the end turned out to the name Uyoma. The origin of the name Uyoma comes from the Omolo's childhood bad games that turned in to the death of the Kawango children and the dismissal of meetings to address these issues or childish games.

Owila the father of Omollo once said, '*Omolo en nyahtina, ok anyal wite, mak mana ka unyisa kama iwite nyithindo…*' Omolo is my son and I cannot throw him away unless you show me a dustbin where children are thrown.

Omolo disappeard during the funerals and disagreements between Jo-Uyoma and Kawango, he reappeared at Alego Kobare in their home today known as gunda Uyoma. This time, Omolo was now grown up and even ready to marry.

The Omolo Ng'o Ng'o character is not strange in Uyoma. From the grazing age for an Uyoma boy, life has two major challenges, the first one is that thou *must fight to survive and grow*. The second challenge is that thou must defend the home and home includes your brothers, sisters and parents plus property especially land and livestock. This training started many generations before Omolo Ng'ong'o was born; this practice is still being practised in Uyoma todate although not as stringent like my time in the late 1950s and 1960s. This training is equivalent to the Madras teaching of the Muslim community which is started from the age of five years to ten years. The Muslims take a clear lead in Religious teaching and training among World Religions.

I remember that as children up to teenage we were always given these tasks whenever I went for holidays in Uyoma. Even today I cherish these responsibilities and they are part and parcel of my life.

ONYANGO WUON OTONDE

Onyango wuon Otonde is from Kakelo of Kabudha clan. He is one of the people who led Jo-Uyoma from Kanyamwa on their return to their ancestral land. He was born in Uyoma and during the movement to Kanyamwa he was a youth.

He is the one who was sent to present the Uyoma case to the female magician *Janyakalondo ma dhako* who demanded from him human waste from an old woman and the offal *wen* of a sheep. Onyango wuon Otonde licked the human waste *Chieth* from an old woman, a ritual that would enable Jo-Uyoma to return safely to their ancestral land. Although Jo-Uyoma would return safely it entailed various hurdles which would involve battles with the current occupants. These rituals would enable Jo-Uyoma to fight, overcome the hurdles and battles infront of them.

Onyango Wuon Otonde and other leaders were sent to the Magician Ogalo wuon Tieng'o and carried out all the instructions and hence Jo-Uyoma returned to their ancestral land'

MOLO NYADUNDO

Molo Nyadundo was a stout short man hence the nick name *Nyadundo*. He comes from Katwenga' clan. Molo was a brave young man who gave his life to Jo-Uyoma in the battle with the British Colonial soldiers at Migowa. He faced the British army that had killed Jo- Uyoma at the OLuoch Abaki's home. The British Colonial forces and their henchmen had raided over four thousand livestock from the Uyoma homes and were now headed for Gem through Asembo. Molo and his team stopped the British with spears and arrows against the well armed trained Colonial officers with guns and horses.this was of the battle of guns verses spears.

Molo and Otieno Osogo led the Uyoma gladiators in battle. Molo speared and killed five men before reaching the British leader on a horse and as he moved to spear him, the British collaborator from Gem known as Ndeda shot him and the bullet hit his left thigh and this sent him to the ground.

The Whiteman on the horse back escaped the wrath of Molo's spear but Molo never stopped the fight until they overwhelmed the British and returned home with 50% of the livestock. Molo bled to death that hot sunny afternoon of 27th December 1899 next to the present CCA Compound in Migowa.

The military onlslaught by the British on Jo- Uyoma brought the loss of great leaders, like OLuoch Abaki and many Uyoma gladiators. The memorable gladiators are; Molo Nyadundo, Obara Kadawo, Otieno Osogo, Malago Pacho, Ogundo Liech, Ragwar, Oluga Dipondo, Malago Kombe, Ogutu Anyieche, Monye, and Agunga Wuon Oyola. The leaders were Aloo Oyuga, Anyiri Kosando, Ongalo Mijuka, Osike Kirina.

The greatest gain of the Mumbo Masscre was the bravery and courage and motivation of Molo Nyadundo that he left for Jo-Uyoma.He remains the greatest gladiator that Uyoma has produced.At death he humbled himself to selflessness for his people and only equated to the Buddhist Dharma *true teaching* on self conquest, **" Though he should conquer a thousand men in the battlefield a thousand times, yet he, indeed, who would conquer himself is the noblest victor"** And so let Molo Nyadundo the gladiator live on in the corridors of the mind of Jo-Uyoma time memorial.

MBOGA WUON OTIENO

Mboga was born in 1840s in Uyoma and he became the fourth traditional Chief from 1880 up to 1899. His mother was from Suba community from Mfangano Island. The Abasuba came from Uganda in 1790; they were rebels in Kabaka Suna's Court. Due to family or sibling disagreement this group moved to Southern Uganda before migrating to Southern Nyanza via Mfangano Islands. The Abasuba maintained the links with their siblings in Uganda.

Through his maternal linkages Mboga developed social and business relationship with the Kabaka of Uganda. He further made friends with the Kawango Kingdom led by Mumia Ashiundu. He had connections with the Kanyamwa where Jo-Uyoma had lived; he had close ties with his maternal relatives in Suba. From the Island of Mfangano, he gatherd wood known as Mvuli that he used to build large boats that could transport goods toUganda.

By the time he became the traditional Chief of Uyoma he was already a wealthy man of means and high social ranking. He had built boats that went to the Kabaka for business; in the process he met the Europeans, the Arabs and people from the Coastal region of Kenya. He knew that the British wanted dominance, he was aware the Kabaka also wanted dominance and protection from the various intruders. The greatest threat was from Egypt, the powerful Pharaoh. Mboga was well versed in business plus Slave trade. Many people claim that he was a slave trade agent for the Arabs through the blessings of the Kabaka of Buganda .He did business with the Kabaka and the Arabs. For the Kabaka, the main commodity that he took to Uganda was soda ash from Huma hills in Karachuonyo. To the Arab slave traders, he collected slaves from Uyoma, Sigulu island, Port Victoria and Ngeta, we can summarise that Mboga collected slaves from the Nyanza Gulf for the Arabs. The evidence of slave trade is clear because I am a victim since my great grandmother Muche Nyar Ajemo was captured at Kunya beach by the slave traders.

From the Kabaka, he got jewels, guns, and other modern household equipments. From the Kabaka, he introduced agricultural commodities such as bananas, fruits and other farm products to Uyoma. The evidence that Mboga had these connections, from the Arab word, he named one of his sons Amadi and from the Kabaka, another son was named Kabaka. The Luos could not pronounce the word Kabaka, so they called Mboga's son Kawaka. Kawaka's home is situated at Kona Kawaka on the road from Bondo heading to Madiany on one side and to Misori and Lwanda Kotieno on the other side.

The Kawango Chief also wanted regional dominance, the region cover a wide area ranging from the current Luhya land (Western Province, Nyanza Province and part of the Rift Valley past Kericho). Mboga needed the chief Ashiundu because the slaves from Uganda could not pass across the current Nyanza to western because there was no protection, so the easiest route to Mombasa was to transport the slaves from Nyanza gulf to Uganda and then through Kawango where they were sure of protection enroute to Mombasa. Nobody in Uyoma had such vast network and knowledge. Mboga's knowledge, wealth and network enabled him to take over the Uyoma leadership. Mboga was actually a people's Chief equivalent to an elected leader. His main ambition was to take over leadership from other Nyanza locations such as Sakwa, Gem, Alego and become another Ashiundu of Kawango.

In history, it is recorded that Mboga predicted the coming of the Whiteman, for Jo-Uyoma. This is not true, Mboga clearly knew about the Whiteman through his connection and network with the Kabaka and the Kawango. He knew their social, economic and political ambitions, their military strength, their missionary agenda and education were well known by Mboga. He clearly warned Jo-Uyoma, but the defiant, proud warriors and warlike Uyoma gladiators and elders did not listen to him.

In his last trip to the Kabaka, he assured the British that Uyoma would comply and work with them. It came to pass when a meeting was held at Othoch Nyamarimba and facilitated by Mboga. This meeting was attended by the Colonial Chiefs and British representatives, the meeting did not work out and there was grave misunderstanding and disagreement that led to physical assault. The meeting broke in disarray and the British never forgave Mboga for this meeting, they promised a military come back and hence the Mumbo Massacre.

Mboga was a big looser, it is his home that the military went to and torched and burnt down literally everything, from structures and animals. Through his inside intelligence he knew the Kawango plan that led to the Mumbo massacre. So by the time the military arrived in Uyoma, Mboga had assembled all his family and movable property in his boats and set them ready to move to Rusinga. While in the Lake he watched the military attack his empty home.

Many people claim that Mboga carried Tse-Tse fly; *maugo* from Uganda that caused the sleeping sickness. It is possible that this could have happened; the same way diseases and virus were transmitted through lugagges and other means.

People also believed that he had magical powers and that he could treat various diseases, influence rainfall and even assist people to acquire wealth or wives..

Later on some of Mboga's family members came back and settled in West Uyoma. Incidentally, Mboga is a strange man and mysterious. It would be good to know more about him. Key informants say that Mboga was able to speak Kiganda, Kiswahili and even some English. Mboga remains one of the most mysterious leaders in Uyoma. To date, nobody is sure where Mboga ended, it could be Uganda, the islands, or even Kawango, but history will tell.

JONATHAN OKWIRI WUOD NYAKINYA

Jonathan Okwiri popualry known as Okwiri Ongutu comes from Kotwal family of Uyoma Kobong'. He was the son of Nyakinya. He was born in 1886.

In 1906 he was the first batch from Uyoma that joined the famous Maseno School and was trained as a teacher at St. Chardwick Teachers' College, Butere. As a teacher, he was elevated to the position of Headmaster of Chianda Sector and Africa Union School in Kisumu. Several notable personalities such as Ramogi Achieng Oneko of Kapenguria Six, Fanuel Walter Odede the Chairman of KAU during the state of Emergency (MAU MAU), Professor Warsau, Dickson Oruko Maka Asembo among others.

Mwalimu/Chief Jonathan Okwiri Nyakinya taken in 1952

Jonathan Okwiri was an articulate British trained Administrator, an eloquent English speaker and well groomed in his dressing. He was a political animal amidst the technocrat training and work; he championed Human Rights especially of the Africans. He was very interested in the Rights of the African people against the authoritarian and discriminative British rule in Luo land before venturing into the national politics. As a person he was known for his bravery which portrayed the characteristic of his forefathers. He often took the White British Administrators head on, a very unheard of thing in those days. He was a great time keeper and was known to outwit many British Administartors for keeping time at any function or appointment. He is remembered for fighting corruption and through out his tenure anything boardering to bribery was not entertained. He hated idlers and nonsense. He loved education and helped many of his relatives to acquire modest education among them was his nephew Richard Arina Oulo Nyakinya who later became a DC, Robert Ngure who became President of African Tribunal Court, Obondo Oulo who was the first African cooperative Officer, Martin Mito Jura who was a teacher and later medical practitioner, Nahason Nyakinya who was a personal assistant to the Provincial Commisioner, Nyanza and Obange Jura who served in the British Intelligence Army in Burma during the World War II

The Luo people elected him as the Chairman in 1922 at Lundha conference in Gem of Buch Piny Owacho (The Voice of the People). Literally translated as "The Voice of the World" "The World has said" 'The people have voiced it". The name was such that you could not pin down any particular person for having said anything against the British Colonial rule.

In an effort to shut him down the British Government offered him a job as the Secretary of Central Kavirondo Local Native Council in 1924. He turned down this offer, because it was a mere clerical job dictated and driven at the whims of the British authority.

In 1940 he was appointed as the Chief of Uyoma upon the demand by the Uyoma people which he gladly took over after Nathan Ojungo. He held this position up to 1952 when he resigned as a protest in sympathy with his relatives Fanuel Odede Obonyo and Achieng Oneko's detention. After his resignation, he ventured into full time politics.

During his life as a teacher, politician and as the Uyoma Chief he championed the following:

- ✓ He advocated for education and encouraged the young to go to school.
- ✓ He facilitated and assisted many people to go to school during his tenure as the Chief of Uyoma
- ✓ He cherished family union and intervened in many family matters to ensure family cohesion both as chief and as an elder
- ✓ He treated Jo-Uyoma as one big clan and dissisted any form of clan discrimination
- ✓ He fought corruption in the Government system and at all levels in the Country. He believed Kenya should be a corruption free Country
- ✓ He lobbied for abolishment of taxation and regularization of the tax system and explained to the people, what tax was required and what tax did to the community
- ✓ He advocated for employment without discrimination, people should be appointed on merit, accademic qualification, required skills not race, tribe or nepotism
- ✓ As the leader of Piny Owacho, he created political linkages at regional level with leaders such as Benjamin Owuor from Sakwa, Ex-Chief Paul Mbuya Akoko from karachuonyo and Omino Ogola from Kisumu.
- ✓ He worked with Ramogi Achieng'Oneko who was publishing the Luo Newspaper known as Ramogi. His objective was to spread the thinking of Piny Owacho
- ✓ He developed linkages with the distant Kikuyu politicians and connected Piny Owacho with Kikuyu Central Association and worked with politicians such as Harry Thuku, Eliud Mathu, Jomo Kenyatta among others

- ✓ He later worked with Kenya African Union (KAU) which was the top most political party in Kenya known all over Africa. Here he worked closely with Kenyan political giants including Harry Thuku, Jomo Kenyatta the Chairman of KAU, Paul Ngei the Treasurer and Achieng Oneko the Secretary General
- ✓ In 1950 he was among the Kenyan dignitaries who visited King George the 6th in Buckingham Palace in Britain.
- ✓ In 1965 he was an official visitor of the Kremlin, in USSR.
- ✓ Brought the idea of starting of Uyoma Polytechnic which is situated in South Uyoma, Naya.

Constituted the Uyoma Water Supply Committee.(pi water ma Uyoma)

The traces of his family members are his two sons Henry Gero Okwiri and Pym Otieno Okwiri.

The family of the late Jonathan Okwiri pausing with the author in the photo

Jonathan Okwiri died in 1978

WALTER FANUEL ODEDE OBONYO

Walter Fanuel Odede was born in 1914. He was the son of Obonyo Akech and Akinyi Nyar Odede from Asembo K-ochieng'. Odede comes from Uyoma Katwenga of Koyoo family. He is known as Rachilo Wuod Obonyo *The black soot the son of Obonyo*

Walter Odede started his education at Chianda Sector (Primary School) and proceeded to Maseno School and then Alliance High School. He later joined Makerere College and graduated with a Diploma in Vetinary Science. After his graduation he took up a job as a lecturer at Makerere College. He is the first Phd holder and Lecturer from Uyoma, infact one of the very few Africans in Kenya and Uganda. Later he was appointed as the first African Principal of Kabete Veterinary School in 1943.

During his tenure as the Principal at Kabete, he was appointed to act as the representative of Africans to the Legislative Council or Kenyan Legislative Assembly holding brief for Bishop Beetcher who was on leave to United Kingdom. It is therefore recorded that he was the first Kenyan to represent Africans in the legislative assembly.

Bishop Beetcher was a good friend and associate of Odede, he advised him to develop his career by going for further studies. Although Beetcher was representing the British Government interest, he saw academic potential in Odede.

The Governor of Kenya Sir Philip Mitchel also took interest in the career development of Mr. Odede. He gave Odede two choices, one to develop his career further by going to Liverpool University and graduate in Veterinary Science or go into politics. Mr. Odede chose to go to Liverpool University, and he became the first person from Uyoma to get a University Degree from a recognized University.

On his return from Liverpool University, Odede went full swing into politics at the disappointment of Colonial Government. He got involved with the KAU leadership.

On 20th October 1952 the KAU leaders were arrested including his kinsman and cousin Ramogi Achieng' Oneko. The others were Jomo Kenyatta, Bildad Kaggia, Kungu Karumba, Fred Kubai and Paul Ngei. Odede took the Chairmanship of Jomo Kenyatta. Nobody believed that anybody would take up KAU leadership at the height of the state of emergency that was declared after the arrest of KAU leaders and activists plus MAU MAU Freedom fighters. He then took major initiatives to fight the unlawfull arrest of KAU and MAU MAU leaders and thousands of activists. Some say that the main motivation was the arrest of his youthfull cousin Ramogi Achieng' Oneko who was by now a fullfledged politician. It is recorded that Achieng Oneko at his youth had lived at Oyieko's family when at Chianda school and had close ties with Odede Obonyo.

Q.C Pritt and Tom Mboya

It did not take long before Odede consulted Argwings Kodhek, the only African practicing lawyer by then who introduced him to his mentor Q.C. D.N. Pritt. Odede travelled to Britain to get an advocate who would represent the Kapenguria Six. The Queens Council (Q.C.) Mr. D.N. Pritt, Davis from Nigeria, A.R.Kapila from the High Court of Kenya did a remarkable legal representation and the KAU leaders were released only later to be re-arrested and detained. Through Odede, Pritt travelled to Uganda by air from Britain and then to Kenya through Kampala Uganda by rail, the then East African Railway Services.

Due to his many political activities and having taken the leadership of KAU, Odede was also detained for five years; March 1954 to 1960.

After his release from detention, Odede became the Chairman of African District Association (ADA) of Central Nyanza, Makasembo was his emissary. ADA was an association that was in place representing political parties which had been banned. He later formed Luo United Movement (LUM)

Fanuel Odede held various non elective political positions and these are:

From 1943 to1944 he represented African interests in Parliament in an acting capacity when Bishop Beecher was on leave in Britain.

From 1952 to 1953 he representd Nyanza in Parliament

From 1961 to 1963 he was a Specialy Elected Member of Parliament

At the dawn of independence in 1963, Odede stood for Parliamentary seat in Kisumu town on KANU ticket and lost to Amir Jamal of Asian origin. The second stab for Parliamentary election was in 1966 when he lost to Oginga Odinga. His third attempt for Parliamentary election was in 1969 when Jaramogi Oginga Odinga's Bondo seat fell vacant following his detention with Ramogi Achieng Oneko and other KPU members who were opposed to Jomo Kenyatta's KANU rule.This time he lost to a political new comer known as Odongo Omamo.

Odede Rachilo wuod Obonyo was known for his bravery and no tolerance for nonsense, he is always remembered for championing education endevour for the people of Uyoma and his development record are as follows:

- He was the first person to build a permanent house in Bondo shopping Centre as a business premise.
- He carried out transport business with buses plying Uyoma, Kisumu and Songoh route.
- He developed modern agriculture in Uyoma, he advocated for acquisition of title deeds and land ownership.
- He promoted commercial farming of maize, ground nuts, millet and other produce and introduced ploughing using tractors.
- He introduced production of sugar cane and cotton as business ventures.
- He is one of the first Africans to venture in commercial sugar cane production in Sugar belt that is Chemelil, Muhoroni and Songor.
- He promoted commercial livestock for business and introduced grade cattle to increase milk production in Uyoma. This is the first time hybrid livestock was introduced both cows and goats.
- He was instrumental in developing Chianda Secondary School, the first primary school and then the first secondary school in Uyoma, Hon Tom Mboya was the first guest of honour in the Chianda fund raising organized by Odede.
- Remnants of his development efforts were sustained by commercial farmers such as Odundo Aduodo and Enos Arara Tinga. Many people in Uyoma have today chosen the Odede path towards more emphasis on development rather than politics and rhetorics. The development in Uyoma in regard to hybrid livestock, construction of shopping centres, individual homes and overall economic development is at its peak.

- I remember Jaduong' Odede clearly in 1969, this was at Tom Mboya's funeral at Lavington Green estate in Nairobi. I went with my father to the funeral, on arrival Odede and my father embraced each other:
- Odede: " Nyakech"
- Achieng': "Rachilo"
- They both concluded in a chorus "Ekaka"

Odede educated his children both boys and girls and that is how Tom Mboya married his Makerere graduate daughter Ambassador Pamela Mboya, his love for education is demonstrated in his children like Dr. Jorry Odede, Dr. Lumumba Odede among others. His wife Sylvia is still alive. His bravery was evident when he confronted the Government administration in Madiany in broad day light on the GSU invasion on Uyoma in 1972. He made similar confrontation with President Jomo Kenyatta and the GSU molestation was stopped immediately.

Unfortunately his development, commercial and political efforts were thwarted by Jaramogi Oginga Odinga who leaned towards social economy with communist influence. Some people from Uyoma claim that Jaramogi Oginga Odinga silently fought Odede or any one from Uyoma who would rival him politically and hence Odede was one of the culprits among others. In 1974 he was nominated by President Jomo Kenyatta as Member of Parliament but unfornately he died in 1975.

Odede left the legacy of *the* possible first Kenyan president for taking over the KAU leadership left vacant after the arrest of Mzee Jomo Kenyatta in 1952.

ENOS ARARA NGODE -'TINGA'

Arara was born in 1920, he hails from Kanyanam, Kabiero, of Katweng'a clan. He was born at Kasiri on the shores of lake Victoria ,then he moved to Mituri where he died in 2014.He had several wives and children one of which served in Bombadeer Brigade of the Kenya Defence Forces.

Arara was educated at Chianda and received training at Bukura Agricultural Institute where he graduated as Agricultural officer specializing in soil conservation.

He graduated as agricultural officer specialized in soil conservation .He later proceeded to Israel for further training in agricultural science .Upon returning from Israel, he joined the government service where he served in various stations as agricultural officer. He later served as the principal of Kopiata village polytechnic until his retirement. He was in the first eleven Uyoma football team which won Burma cup in 1954.He was a great wrestler who could not be grounded on the floor .He strongly believed in work for cash and could not dish out cash to anybody without one working for it. He was extremely strict and a displinarian. Although he was a polygamous man ,he cooked his own meals at his cottage (*abila*) .He is being admired for his hard work and was a strict disciplinarian .Arara was called Tinga because he encouraged the use of tractor plough instead of oxen plough .He brought modern Agricultural equipments in the 1940s and 1950s years in Uyoma.

RAMOGI ACHIENG ONEKO

Ramogi Achieng Oneko was born in 1920 in Uyoma Kabudha, Kunya Kosewe, *Kunya nindgi lepi* (as he used to say).

He was the son of Oneko Nyauchi (*Sungura*) and Doris Ongala (*Nya-Asila*)

He went to Okela and Chianda Sector. During his early school in Chianda he lived with Arun Njago near Chianda. Harun Njago and Oneko Nyauchi went to World War I and hence the friendship and the love for education. He later joined Maseno Secondary school. His notable teachers were Carey Francis, Jonathan Okwiri, Okelo Ja-kasagam and Oginga Odinga who was also his House master.

He worked as a clerk with the Metrological Department (*near Dagoretti Corner*) for 2 years and resigned unceremoneously due to inhumanizing conditions of the Africans by the Colonial Government. He immediately ventured into business and was one of the very few Africans to open a shop at the Nairobi City Market. By 1946 he was a fullfledged journalist and established Ramogi Newspaper.

He was appointed as a City Commissioner or Councillor in 1945 to 1947 and he is on record for having been instrumental for the constructution of the ledgendary Woodley Estate where he later owned and lived in until his death in 2007 and it remained a family house. The Estate still has the memory of the following families Otieno Ambala, Onyango Midika, Wayaki Wambaa, Ndolo Ayah, Odinge Odera, Luke Obok, Jaduong Yaya and his brother Ogola, Dr.Barrack Obama, Dr. William Ouko, Konchela, Nick Ajuoga, Shipiri, Akatsa, Dr. Joseph OLuoch, The Kenyatta family among others.

During his journalism career he worked with Jaramogi Oginga Odinga, and was instrumental in introducing Odinga to Jomo Kenyatta and other politicians from other tribes.

From Uyoma perspective, he created linkages between the Luos and Kikuyus for the struggle of independence. He specifically introduced Jonathan Okwiri the leader of *Piny Owacho* to Harry Thuku and Eliud Mathu and later to national stage for political agitation.

He later became the General Secretary of KAU and together with Koinange he tabled Kenya's desire for independence at the Congress of People Against Imperialism to be forwarded to the United Nations

General Assembly in London in January 1952. He is remembered dearly among the Kikuyu in Nyeri for supporting MAU MAU and his statement from Britain was "The Tree of Freedom is watered with blood'. The Colonial Government never forgave him.

He is among the Kapenguria Six who were detained in 1952 for the MAU MAU movement. The Kapenguria Six are Jomo Kenyatta, Bildad Kaggia, Kungu Karumba, Fred Kubai, Paul Ngei Achieng' Oneko. They were detained and Oneko spent almost ten years in Prison and Detention.

His detention motivated Jo-Uyoma to agitate for Kenya's Independence.

On his release in 1961 he became a Personal Assistant and Secretary to Jomo Kenyatta. During this time he was instrumental in sending several youths from Uyoma for education to Europe, which included Russia, Romania, Yugoslavia, Bulgaria and East Germany among others.

In 1963, he won the Nakuru Parliamentary seat and became the Minister for Information Broadcasting and Tourism

In 1963, He was elected Member of Parliament for Nakuru and appointed Minister for Broadcasting, Information, Tourism and Wildlife. After the infamous Limuru Conference of 1966. Achieng' Oneko resigned from the government against President Jomo Kenyatta's wish and joined Jaramogi Oginga Odinga to form opposition party KPU (*Kenya Peoples Union*) and he lost his Nakuru seat and became General Secretary of KPU.

He became Chairman of Rothman, a tobacco setup and ran a wholesale business in Nairobi and Kisumu.

From his second detention, he ventured into business; he was appointed the Chairman of Kenya Film Co-operation by President Moi and later started fishing business with Odeny Ngure. In 1983 he contested the Langata Parliamentary seat and lost to Philip Leakey in disputed election results.

In 1988 he supported Jalang'o Nyanduga to outwit the strong and popular Siaya KANU Chairman Ouma Okendo to take up the Rarieda Parliamentary seat.

He was part of Kenya's third liberation and joined FORD, Later FORD-Kenya and served as the National Treasurer until 2007. In 1992, he was elected MP for Rarieda constituency and during his tenure he was elected the chair of Inter Party Parliamentary Group (IPPG) that brought some changes in the Kenya's constitution before the 1997 General Elections.

He promoted the Kunya Dispensary, Achieng Oneko Secondary School, Chairman of Nyamasore Secondary School, and the Rageng'ni-Kunya road. Jointly with Hon Raphael Tuju and Ongalo they initiated the Uyoma tarmac road network, electricity and other Uyoma infrastractural initiatives.

He remained in active politics serving as the FORD – KENYA National Treasurer until his demise in 2007.

During his interaction with Rev. Jack Owenda, he said "Lets wait and see if a quail climbs a tree" "*wananeye ka Aluru oidho yath…*" He said this while referring to the Luo mass exodus from the Kibaki government in 2005.

He was later detained in 1969 upto 1975 and sets record as Kenya's longest political detainee (16 years in detention) and only second to Nelson Mandela (27 years) on the African soil. Achieng Oneko is the longest serving politician (64s years) spanning from 1943 to 2007, from a tender age of 25 years to the age of 87 years and through many political turbulances. The man has along story.

Achieng Oneko and his family

Nyakech tiende tindo, Nyakech Oluoro chuodho

Oluoch Okelo "Owando Kwach, Kwach ger, Mande imulo kose tho"

Ondiek Chilo, Owad gi Oyaro.

One day in 1977, I confronted my Father and I told him, 'I am tired of the opposition, why don't you drop your friendship with Jaramogi Oginga Odinga, so that our business can grow and stop wallowing in poverty? I told him, 'Our business cannot thrive if we cannot get the seating Government goodwill. He looked at me very politely while he was calm, cool and collected, he told me, 'my son you were born in Nairobi go hee to the streets of Nairobi and search for an Angel if you find one call me'. Then I understood why he kept the long lasting relationship with Jaramogi Oginga Odinga and warm relationship with Mzee Jomo Kenyatta. Friends and lovers are for keeps not for kicks. From that day todate I keep my friends because I have travelled the world and I have never met an Angel.

He died on the 9th June 2007 and was given a state burial which was attended by H.E Mwai Kibaki, The Former President Daniel Moi and The Former Prime Minister Raila Amolo Odinga, Chairman of FORD- Kenya Muskari Kombo, Former Attorney General Charles Mugane Njonjo amongst many dignitaries. The Masters of Ceremonies were led by James Ogundo and assisted by Omamo Kodande and Odiwuor Nyassio.

He left the legacy of the most possible second vice president and later president if he did not join Jaramogi Oginga Odinga's pressure to quit the government as the minister for information from the then KANU kitchen cabinet led by Tom Mboya and Charles Njonjo.

RICHARD ARINA OULO.

Richard Arina Oulo was born in 1910, his father is Oulo Nyakinya, he hails from the family of Kotwal of kobong' clan. He is also known as Arina DC. He is Jonathan Okwiri's nephew and was brought up and grew up in Maseno School compound.

He attained his education in Maseno School and then he proceeded to Alliance High School. He later went to Makerere and earned a diploma in Administration and economics.

From 1937 to 1945 he was the Headteacher of Maseno School; by 1946 he was appointed District Commisssioner (DC). He is recorded as the first African DC in Kenya. As a DC he worked in various Districts such as Kakamega, Kisii, Rongo and Migori among others.

It is alledged that Arina DC was poisoned after completing his course to be promoted to the post of a provincial commissioner. He married Alice Nyar Yimbo, his children were Jamwa, Bob Jalango', and Atieno. He died in 1964.

GIDEON OGUDE NYAORO

Ogude was born in 1900. He was from the Kajore clan. He was educated at Maseno and Native Industrial Training Centre in Kabete. He was trained as a dressmaker and later on roads construction.

He started tailoring in Kisumu and later he was elected to represent Uyoma in the Local Native Council of Central Kavirondo in 1925. He initiated Uyoma water project which was accepted in 1938 but was delayed due to the World War Two. Later in 1949 funds were availed for water and water pans and dams were built in Uyoma.

Ogude is also remembered for having approached Bishop Owen in 1934 to change his mind of removing Okela sector school to Kano after the school had been burnt down. He also argued this case with the central Kavirondo DC Mr. Hunter *Handa* that Uyoma children could not travel to Kano unless it was a boarding School. In 1951 he was appointed the roads supervisor of class C 28 He foresaw the contruction of Ruma-Gagra-Chianda-Rageng'ni -Lweya - Ndigwa Road. He was later appointed Roads Supervisor for central Nyanza. In 1963 he contested the Uyoma councillorship against Mr.William Nyawanda Obonyo and was defeated.

Ogude is remembered for his courage and love for Uyoma and intelligence, he is survived with several children amongst them JP Kogude, Prof. Adera Ogude .FF. Okwiri Ogude.Many many many People are named after Ogude. He died in 1968

DICKSON ORUKO MAKASEMBO

Dickson Oruko Makasembo was born in 1917 and his father was known as Asembo Kokoth. Maka means belonging to or son of hence Makasembo which also means son of Asembo.

Oruko was known by his peers as *Owad gi Agutu, Nyang' wange' chiegni gi dho loo*. Oruko the brother of Agutu, the crocodile whose eyes are close to the ground, this means that he was furious as a crocodile.

He was educated at Chianda Sector and Kagwa Sector *Primary School*. Later he joined Kamagambo Mission School.

Oruko lived a hyper active life during his school life but managed to complete his education. With his erratic life he got a job in a Christian Missionary School as a teacher in Nakuru, where he worked for less than two years. The Missionary community was not happy with his life style which involved dancing and playing guiter after his school engagements. These nocturnal activities were viewed as anti-Christian and Oruko was relieved of his early teething teaching profession.

After his failed teaching career, Oruko was recruited into the World War II in 1939 as a soldier where he worked for two years. At the end of the war after deployment Oruko went to Kisumu town and returned to his music life with comrades such as Laban Abonyo and Odero Achume. He got a job with a company called Unga; again this work was short lived. In early part of 1950 Oruko got a job that befitted him and which would later propel him to national prominence. The job he got was a casual job of selling two newspapers one known as Baraza and the other one was Ramogi. Ramogi was run by Ramogi Achieng' Oneko who hailed from Uyoma like him. Oruko made enormous sales of the newspapers due to his public relations and his Kisumu fame for music. Within a matter of months various newspapers recruited him as a news correspondent. From a mere newspaper vender in Kisumu, he started travelling in the whole of Nyanza collecting and disseminating news and he joined the ranks of those agitating for Kenya's Independence. These activities suited Oruko due his hyper active life; he worked for Piny Owacho Newspaper which published Nyanza Times. Soon Oruko ran into trouble with the authorities and was jailed for nine months together with comrade Were

The home and grave tomb of the late Senator Dickson Oruko Makasembo in Kamariga, Kagwa, West Uyoma

After the Piny Owacho, he joined other political movements that formed KANU, Oruko fought for party leadership in Nyanza, and defeated Ochwada and he became the Chairman of KANU in Nyanza.

At the dawn of Kenya's Indendence in 1963 Oruko battled for a national position and that was the post of Senator in Nyanza. He lobbied for support and campaigned in the whole of Nyanza and he was elected as the first Senator in Central Nyanza.

Oruko was a tough, brave man who championed political agitation during the British Colonial rule that suppressed political movements and activities in Kenya. He also cherished education. He initiated Makasembo Secondary School in 1963. In 1964 while President Jomo Kenyatta visited Achieng' Oneko in Uyoma Oruko took advantage and organized a fundraising *Harambee* for the school. The President donated Ksh. 20,000 while Jaramogi Oginga Odinga (The Vice President) and Achieng Oneko (*The Minister for Information*) both donated Ksh.10, 000 each. This is the foundation of the present Makasembo Secondary School in Uyoma.

Oruko Makasembo died prematurely in a road accident on 11th December 1965.

I personally remember the occasion. We had gone to Jamhuri Park and as our driver Ben Ochanda was waiting to pack, a group of people met my father and the information was as follows in Luo " *Jaduong' wan ka, to, Oruko to onge*" "Oldman we are here but Oruko is no longer with us.

The pre-Jamhuri celebration for us had an anti-climax as I saw my mother, Jedidah pull out a handkerchief and weep.

MBOGO OKELLO

Mbogo Okelo Wuod Mandera *Chiel wiye Oke* (The jagged hedge or fence) *okew kagwa* was the son of Joshua Okelo who went to Maseno school together with John Odande and Mama Mandera. This man lived a full dramatic life surpassing Omolo Ong'ong'o but made many undocumented incidences in the History of Uyoma.

He was a highly educated man from the famous Chianda and Maseno Schools but was notorious in the opposition of the Colonial administration. At regional level in 1959 he led the *Kisumu naked demonstration.* Since KAU was banned in 1952 KANU was formed in 1958 to replace KAU. The main symbol of KANU was red T-Shirts which KANU leaders and activists used to wear especially at their rallies and other forums. The KANU activists were not allowed to wear these red T-Shirts. The KANU activists in Kisumu led by Mbogo Okelo held the demonstration telling the Colonialist that they did not need to wear the clothes they introduced in Kenya including T-Shirts and trousers. The demonstrators stripped stuck naked and handed the clothes to Odundo Nyar Ouma from Uyoma Rabel; she was the sister of Chief Ogol of Uyoma. Her duty was to carry the clothes and when they reached the Government offices she would throw the clothes infront of the Nyanza D.C.s office. The District Commissioner was Mr. Pedrassa. The demands of the demonstrators included the following:

- KANU activists should be allowed to wear their KANU red T-Shirts at all their functions
- KANU should be given a licence to hold rallies and popularize the KANU vision and objectives
- Mzungu should go back to their Country

The demonstration entailed walking naked in the main street of Kisumu from Chiro Mbero to the DCs office.

When they reached the DCs office, Auma moved to the front line and threw the clothes infront of the DC and told him that " We have brought back the Whiteman's clothes" ' Today men have come to you naked the women will come tomorrow naked" *"Kawuono chuo obironi duge kiny mon nobi duk thiring'inyi"*

The DC and his other Government officers could not believe what they witnessed infront of their offices; the naked crowd was over fifty people. Posing bluntly and shamelessly infront of the DC was Mbogo Okelo the Team leader, the other people from Uyoma were Omil Kokokola from Kajore, Mariko Odipo from Kagwa, Ochido Alindi from Kabudha, Otuoma Ooro from Kabudha, Abonyo Oyombe from Kagwa, Omolo Arambe from Nyakach, Were Olonde and Mito Jura from Kobong'. Among the naked demonstrators was Abonyo Oyombe .The other demonstrators from other places were Owino Abuoro from karachuonyo, Owuor Kamaundu from Seme, Naman Akumu from Nyakach, Rasamba from Alego, Zedi Kobiero Ja Matangwe, Olenyo from Asembo, Ombok Thim from Alego, Omoro Onono from Kano, Ywaya Odero from Asembo.

The DC granted them permission to hold rallies and other forums immediately to avoid embarrassment of the British Government among its European and World peers. Worst of all was the embarrassment to the Queen of England especially after the notice from Odundo nyar Ouma, that women would be coming naked the next day.

The next day they appeared in court naked and they all were set free.

Mbogo was Chief Uhuru for Uyoma; he was a temporary secretary of Amoth Owira the Chief of Alego. It is important to note that Mbogo Okelo at one of the DCs Barazas in Madiany, he confronted the White DC and told him that children or boys of his calibre' are not allowed to smoke a pipe infront of adults and especially in public. The DO of Bondo Isaac Okwiri was very annoyed with Mbogo's remarks and the Jo-Uyoma negative reaction. He asked his askaris, administrative security personnel to arrest Mbogo immediately. The law enforcers were stopped by the Uyoma Baraza participants who stood up in support of their son Mbogo, they forcefully stopped the arrest. The next day Mbogo was put under house arrest in his home in Kunya Ka-Osewe and guard. Mbogo constantly confronted the administrative guards while naked and smeared them with feaces. Mbogo asked the guards to vacate his home; his rescue came from Jo-Kunya. The youth of Kunya Ka-Osewe confronted the the Administrative guards and they got a proper Kunya beating and ran for their lives up to Bondo.While Mbogo was under house arrest a state of emergency was declared on the defiant Uyoma, a reign of Johny terror was unleashed upon Jo-Uyoma. The *Majoni* an equivalent to the current General Service Unit (GSU) the Government security used unorthodox thuggery against Jo-Uyoma and many men were wounded and maimed, while women were raped scores upon scores.

This action was not just because of Mbogo but the DO Okwiri comes from Gem and it is said he was revenging old scores. It was also common knowledge then that the authority had always wanted an excuse to discipline Jo-Uyoma because of their constant political activities against the Colonial Government. These activities included Achieng Oneko's and Odede's KAU national leadership and MAU MAU association, apart from the above personalities, the other defiant leaders like Jonathan Okwiri, Makasembo and the known Uyoma's history of defiance.

Mbogo, Adhiambo Wamola, Oyaro Oneko, Odundo Wanyadha among many Uyoma political activists were at that time supporters of Odede in preference to Oginga Odinga from the neighbouring Sakwa.

Omolo Arambe from Nyakach who is one of the naked demonstartors is the original founder of the national slogan Harambee. He used to lead the other KANU activists in various team works, activities and participatory tasks, and as he led the task, other team members would shout the word Arambe and hence the formation of the slogan Harambee. Today fundraising functions in Kenya are known as harambee, President Jomo Kenyatta promoted the team effort through the slogan of harambee and other politicians followed suite to date and it became a national slogan of *"Pooling and pulling resources together"*.

Later on in life Mbogo made a repeat behavior against the man he supported most and it was none other than the then President Jomo Kenyatta. It happened that Mbogo had paid Ksh. 1000 as nomination fees for Bondo Parliamantery seat and was denied a ticket. This forced Mbogo to confront Kenyatta naked with additional smearing of *shit on* his naked body. When the President was alerted he ordered the refund of this money to avoid further embarrassment from the man he knew very as a staunch KANU supporter and further more a nephew of his long standing political comrade Ramogi Achieng' Oneko.

Mbogo Okello was always viewed as a mad or insane person yet this is not true. The writer of this book is a relative of Mbogo and confesses that his cousin Mbogo was a sane man with academic excellence, intelligent man who was widely read and well informed.

He served as a clerk in the Judiciary and was well versed with legal issues. Mbogo was very philanthropic and could be remembered for dishing out money especially in Rageng'ni Market. He was generous and donated clothings to the widows and orphans. He aped Alladin of England who used to rob the rich and donate to the poor, he also admired Robinhood stories.

He started his own religious sect called Ramogi. He opposed the western system of religion the so-called Christianity that took him to school. He instead wanted an African and to be specific, a Luo based religion which would promote the Luo culture and values. His sect was very sympathetic to the deprived members of the society such as widows, orphans, the disabled and the insane among others.

EDWIN ONYANGO RADIER

Edwin Onyango Radier was born in 1940 in Yimbo. He was the son of Mr. and Mrs Radier.

Edwin and his mother Okaka, relocated to Uyoma after the death of his father Radier in 1945, to stay with his paternal uncle Malowa wuon Okoth who was a very wealthy man amongst the Kagwala of Kagwa clan in Uyoma.

In 1948 Edwin went to live with his sister Alice Ademba in Kaloleni Kisumu. Amongst the notable tenants there were Apollo Ohanga, a member of LEGCO, Jaramogi Oginga Odinga who was a businessman, Ramogi Achieng Oneko and their landlord, Mr. Albert Awino Olal, who was the treasurer of African District Council of Central Nyanza.

After completing his KAPE, he worked with the catholic bookshop in Nairobi and later resigned to become a political activist. In 1960 he joined the naked demonstration against the colonial government led by Dickson Mbogo Okello and Were Olonde. He was arrested and jailed together with Were Olonde from Nyakach, Nyamolo Miyawa of Kano, Ajumbo Owino of Kisumu, Arwenyo Kunga of Kano, Abor Rono of Seme, and John Migot Awuor of Seme for three months.

On the day of their release from jail, there was a massive demonstration to welcome them back to the society and in the process, the Kodiaga main prison gate was destroyed because of the jubilation. This destruction of the only gate led to major changes in the construction of security gates in the whole of Kenya. Today, in Kenya, every prison has two to four gates.

He served as a personal assistant to Jaramogi Oginga Odinga which gave him chance to meet some of the Kenyan freedom agitators. Amongst them Jomo Kenyata, Thomas Joseph Mboya, Ronald Ngala, Masinde Muliro, Jeremiah Nyaga.

After Kenya attained her self internal government in 1963, he was offered a special scholarship to the then Union of Soviet Socialist Repulic (USSR) to study for a diploma in public administration in anticipation of recruitment in independent government.

Upon return from his studies in USSR in 1965, his team was branded communists and could not be absorbed in the President Jomo Kenyatta's government as they were inclined to Jaramogi Oginga Odinga and Achieng' Oneko.

He was elected as a councilor representing central ward in Kisumu municipality where he served alongside notable personalities like Grace Onyango M.P, Mathews Ondiek Omondi, Samson Odoyo, James Miruka Owuor, John Onyango Otieno, Asiko Obare and S.M.Otieno. He was very instrumental in the establishment of Mama Ngina Hostel during his councillorship.

In 1969, there was a lot of political tension in Kenya after the assacinations of Argwins Kodhek, Tom Joseph Mboya, formation of KPU (DUME) and the opening of Soviet Union Funded New Nyanza General Hospital by president Jomo Kenyatta and subsequent deaths and detention of likes of Jaramogi Oginga Odinga, Ramogi Achieng Oneko, Luke Obok, Wasonga Sijeyo, Ondiek Chilo, Bildad Kaggia, added salt to the sour relationship between the Luos and the Jomo Kenyatta's government.

The same year, Little General Elections was called and Onyango Radier was barred from contesting since he was a KPU sympathizer. Mama Grace Onyango was fronted to contest the parliamentary seat for Kisumu town and won.

Onyango Radier returned to politics during the advent of Multi party democracy in Kenya known as second liberation and in 1992, was elected as a councilllor on a Ford Kenya ticket in Kaloleni Ward Kisumu. He became deputy mayor of Kisumu town upto1997. In 2002, he served as the treasurer NARC Nyanza Council of Elders- Nyanza Branch.

At the time we were publishing this book, the following were the only surviving regional independent freedom fighters from Uyoma; Edwin Onyango Radier, Mariko Odipo, Otuoma Abila, Anyumba Nyamor, Kere Wuon Odhil and Milewa Osemba.

HENRY OUMA OKENDO

Hon. Ouma Okendo was born in 1936. He was educated at Chianda School. He served as a teacher before joining politics and rising to the prestigious position of Siaya District KANU Chairman, at this time, this was an extremely powerful position during the Moi's regime. He also served as Chairman of Siaya County Council a position equivalent to the current Gorvernor of Siaya County. He was elected Uyoma Councillor in 1979 until the time he vied for the Rarieda Parliamentary seat which he lost to the youthful Jalang'o Nyanduga in 1988; He also lost the same seat in 1992 to the elderly veteran politician Ramogi Achieng Oneko. His last political venture was in 1997 against Hon. Odeny Ngure an NDP political giant and an ally of the then power house known as Hon, Raila Amolo Odinga, who later became the Prime Minister of Kenya.

Through his political life Hon. Ouma Okendo remains one of the most philanthropic politicians in Uyoma, he supported many development projects such Uyoma helper project in Madiany. He championed education of the orphaned and less fortunate students both from within and without Uyoma.

He will be remembered as the industrious politician regardless of his position; even at the time Uyoma did not elect him as their MP he remained a stounch supporter of development projects and KANU.

ODENY NGURE

Odeny was born in 1942 in Kotwal of Kobong' clan, he is the son of Ngure Oulo. He is a nephew to the great chief and politician Jonathan Okwiri Nyakinya. He went to Maseno School and later joined the University of Reading in the UK. He is the first quantity surveyor from Uyoma and joined the ranks of the first quantity surveyors in Kenya. Odeny Ngure is self made technocrat and later a leading politician. His political interest was first shown while at Maseno School at the height of the original opposition struggle of KPU in the early1960s. He later went into practice as a quantity surveyor.He remained an active politician alongside his professional carreer it is recorded that he worked very closely with the long standing politician Ramogi Achieng Oneko, he supported him against the contest with Richard Leaky in Langata constituency during the KANU regime in 1983. They both supported Jalang'o Nyanduga to become the first MP for Rarieda 1988; he later supported Ramogi Achieng Oneko to become the second MP for Rarieda in1992. He later worked closely with Raila Amolo Odinga a leading politician in NDP, LDP and ODM. He is recorded to be the founder member of all these three political parties. Odeny became the MP for Rarieda on an NDP ticket in1997. During his political carreer, he promoted several development projects and academic endavours. His wife Pamela Ngure is the current Nominated member of county assembly in Siaya from Uyoma. He passed on in 2012.

MRS. PAMELA ARWA MBOYA

She is a graduate from Makerere University in the 1960s, being the first woman graduate from Uyoma and Nyanza. She is the daughter to the Freedom fighter Fanuel Walter Odede and wife to the World reknowned politician Thomas Joseph Adhiambo Mboya.She served in various high profile positions in Kenya and finaly she was the Permanent Representative to the UN habitat.

MS ELIZABETH ONGORO AMOLO

She was born in Chianda village and is locally refferd to as Nya-chianda or nyar gi Yawuoyi. Elizabeth is the sister to renowned lawyer, Paul Otiende Amollo.

She is a graduate from the University of Nairobi in 1980s. She ventured into business before becoming MP for Kasarani in Nairobi in 2007 and an Assistant Minister. She climbed the political ladder to become the second Senator from Uyoma after Dickson Oruko Makasembo.

She is the deputy secretary general of ODM.

MR. CHADWICK ADONGO KISIRA

Adongo Kisira from Uyoma Katweng'a fought his way from Trade Union to become Deputy Mayor of the vast and cosmopolitan Nairobi City from 1983 to 1988.

He is a leading Trade Unionist, the other great and long serving Uyoma Trade Unionist is Jacob Ochino Ogundo.

MRS JAEL ORIWA ONEKO

Mrs Oneko worked as a civil servant with humble beginings in Siaya Council and turned tables round to venture into politics as a Councillor of Siaya Town then rose to become the fisrt woman Mayor of Siaya Municipal Council. She is the second female Mayor in Nyanza and Western Kenya apart from Mama Grace Onyango who was the fisrt female Mayor in Kisumu

MS PRISCA AUMA MISACHI

She served as a Councillor, Mayor and a Ward Representative in the competitive Kisumu Municipal Council now Kisumu County'. Today she is a Member of County Assembly in Kisumu.

MR. GEORGE ISAIAH OUSA

George Isaiah Ousa the son of Ogutu Muberi was born in 1948 amongest the Kasiemba clan in Naya South Uyoma. He was elected in 1992 on a FORD – KENYA ticket to represent the greater East Uyoma and was subsequently re elected in 1997 on a NDP ticket to represent South Uyoma in the council.

Isaiah Ousa as he is fondly known was instrumental in the establishment of Mayange, Kadiala, Kogowe and Kamin Oningo Beaches as well as Naya Secondary Schools.

He is now doing business from Lwanda Kotieno beach.

DR. PAUL MUYA OTIENDE AMOLLO

Dr. Paul Otiende Amollo was born in chianda in 1972 to Mr. and Mrs. Amollo Samba and Gladys Amollo. Otiende comes from kabiero of Katweng'a clan. He went to Chianda primary school where he passed and joined the prestigious Maranda high school, before proceeding to the University of Nairobi to study law. His home is directly opposite Chianda primary school in Uyoma.

Otiende has held various senior leadership positions both at national and international levels. He was the chair of commission of Jurists Kenya chapter, served as a member of the committee of experts which drafted the Kenya new constitution 2010.

He is the first Kenyan obundsman (the chairman of the commission of administration of justice). He is the president of the obundsman in Africa.

He was awarded an honorary doctorate degree by the Maseno University. He is a potential political animal.

The Uyoma chiefs have been listed here below; the listing entails the time and duration in office, their clan and the highlights of their achievements. It is recorded in History that by 1800, the Luos in Kenya were well established with their Government and social structures in place. The notable Uyoma *Ruodhi* are documented as from 1830 up to the period this book covers which is 1970.

The table is divided into three major periods in the history of Uyoma and these are the Pre-Colonial era, Colonial rein and the dawn of independence.

NO.	CHIEFS/ LEADERS	PERIOD	CLAN	HIGHLIGHT OF ACHIEVEMENTS
	PRE-COLONIAL	**1800-1900**		**INSTALLED BY COMMUNITY BY VIRTUE RECONIZED ACHIEVEMENTS**
1	Onyango Wuon Otonde	1830-1850	Kabudha	Led Uyoma on exodus from Kanyamwa to ancestral land
2	Oguta Wauga	1850-1870	Katwenga'	Leader of Jo-Uyoma in Kanyamwa. Donated sacrificial bull for the return to ancestral land
3	Oginga Agidhi	1870-1880	Katwenga'	Leader when Jo-Uyoma fought and removed (Isembo) Jo-Kale and Sakwa (Sakni) out of Uyoma Settlement of internal Uyoma clan boudaries Setting boundary with Asembo and sakwa
4	Mboga Otieno	1880-1899	Kokwiri	Leader during Colonial invasion of Uyoma Predicted the coming of the whiteman and was involved in slave trade. Poor clan relatioships Had network with Kabaka in Uganda and Mumia in Kawango. Instrumental in the coming of Tse-tse fly
5	Haya Ngode	1899-1900	Kabudha	Short lived leadership, was betrayed by Otumba and did not travel to be appointed in Mumias Too many sibling and clan wrangles Mumbo massacre during his reign

	COLONIAL	1900-1963		**APPOINTED AND INSTALLED BY COLONIAL ADMINISTRATION**
1	Otumba Mbede	1900-1917	Katwenga'	Settling and marking boundary between Sakwa and Asembo. Construction of Aram-Ndigwa Road. Promotion of education Introduced Sisal and groundnuts
2	Paul Moyi Okweso	1917-	Wagoro	Spoke fluent Kiswahili.

			1922		Introduced beddings/blankets and clothes Construction of Owimbi-Misori road
3	Jonathan Otumba Ojungo		1922-1940	Katwenga'	Son of Otumba Mbede. A great sportsman, concerned with family cohesion and Started Chianda School Promoted education sent the following to Maseno: Malaki Odindo, Achieng Oneko and Odede. Settled Kobong'/Katwenga'a boundary
4	Jonathan Okwiri		1940-1952	Kobong'	An administrative guru and promoted time management Promoted Piny Owacho and linkages to national politics He resigned to demonstrated solidarity with his former students i.e Oneko & Odede, KAU. He is recorded as the most political Chief
5	Bathlomeow Nyabola Owiti		1952-1955	Kokwiri	Trained administrator from Kabete Promoted education and Colonial rule Moved Chiefs camp from Owimbi to Manyuanda
6	lijah OLuoch Atipa		1955-1960	Katwenga'	Moved Chiefs camp from Manyuanda to the centre of Uyoma in Madiany Was forced out of office due to defiance of authority by Jo-Uyoma hence Majoni
	THE DAWN OF INDEPENDENCE				**APPOINTED THROUGH INTERVIEWS BASED ON EDUCATION**
1	Samuel Nyawanda		1960-1964	Kabudha	Professional teacher Resisted corruption and clanism Served during the 1st Majoni invasion Was retired prematurity due into clan wrangles
1	Henry Onditi Achola		1964-1988	Katwenga'	Great sportsman and musician, played in football team that brought the Burma Cup to Uyoma in 1954 Instrumental in starting schools such as Chianda, Ndigwa, Madiany and Gagra Secondary Schools. He served at the height of 2nd Majoni onslaught in 1972

THE LATER CHIEFS

	NAME	PERIOD	AREA
1	**Elisha Aggai Angira**	1974 - 1988	West Uyoma
2	**Abisalom Rabala Ojwang'**	1988- 1998	West Uyoma
3	**Oscar Awuolia**	1998to date	West Uyoma
4	**Henry Onditi Achola**	1974- 1988	East Uyoma

5	Casmiel oyaro Okuogo	1988- 1992	East Uyoma
6	Dan Okuma Nange	1992 – 1998	East Uyoma
7	Henry Ouko Otieno	1998-2007	East Uyoma
8	Charles Jomo Ajwang	2007 to date	East Uyoma
9	Casmiel Oyaro Okuogo	1992- 2007	South Uyoma
10	Steven Denge Oliech	2007 to date	South Uyoma
11	Marcel Were Onjara	1998 - 2005	Central Uyoma
12	Cosmas Onyango Okwama	2005 to date	Central Uyoma

PARLIAMENTARY REPRESENTATIVES

No	Name	Constituency	Period
1	Ramogi Achieng Oneko	Nakuru town	1963 -1966
2	Fanuel odede Obonyo	nominated	1974-1975
3	Ramogi Achieng oneko	Rarieda	1992 -1997
4	Odeny Ngure	Rarieda	1997 – 2002
5	Reuben ndolo	Makadara	2002 - 2007
6	Elizabeth Ongoro	Kasarani	2007- 2013

SENATORS

	NAME	CONSTITUENCY	PERIOD
1	Dickson Oruko Makasembo	Central nyanza	1963 -1965
2	Elizabeth Ongoro	Nominated	2013- to date

UYOMA COUNCILLORS AND MEMBERS OF COUNTY ASSEMBLY

COLONIAL COUNCILLORS

No	Name	Area	Period
1	Oluga Nange	Uyoma (DNC)	1920-1924
2	Gideon Ogude Nyaoro	Uyoma (DNC)	1924 – 1929
3	Ramogi Achieng Oneko	Nairobi	1945-1947

Councillors

1	Richard Ochido Alindi	Uyoma	1957-1963
2	Nyawanda Obonyo	Uyoma	1963-1974
3	Jacob Ochino Ogundo	Maringo –nairobi	1963- 1979
4	Henry Ouma Okendo	Uyoma	1974-1988
5	Henry Onditi Achola	East madiany	1988-1992
6	Obunga Elisha	nominated	1988-1992

7	Haggai Angira	West Madiany	1988-1992
8	Onyango Atana	West Uyoma	1992-1997
9	Isiah Ousa	East Madiany	1992-1997
10	Amimo Debogo	Central Uyoma	1992-1997
11	Oscar ochieng Adhiambo	nominated	1997-2002
12	James Omburo Okello	East Uyoma	1997-2002
13	Samuel Ayoki Nyawanda	South Uyoma	1997-2002
14	KenyattaArunda	East Uyoma	1997-2002
15	Amimo Debogo	Central Uyoma	1997-2002
16	Charles Omolo Kowi	East Madiany	2002-2007
17	Dalmas Orwa Midega	West Madiany	2002-2007
18	Prisca Auma Misachi	Kisumu-kaloleni	2002 – 2013
19	John Miraa Mirambe	South Uyoma	2008-2013
20	Dick Oruko Chiama	West Uyoma	2008-2013
21	Grace Alindi (Died in Office)	Central Uyoma	2008-2009
22	James Odhiambo Munda	Central Uyoma	2009 -2013
23	Charles Omolo Kowi	East Uyoma	2008-2013
1	Mathews Odeny Onduru	West Uyoma	2013- to date
2	Charles Omolo Kowi	North Uyoma	2013-to date
3	Christopher Apiyo Apiyo	South Uyoma	2013 to date
4	Prisca Auma Misachi	Kaloleni, kisumu	2013to date
5	Maxwel Adera Ochar	Gomongo –Nairobi	2013 To Date

MAYORS AND DEPUTIES

No	NAME	AREA	PERIOD
1	Charles Adongo Kisira (Deputy Mayor)	Nairobi	1983 - 1988
2	Henry Ouma Okendo (county council chairman)	Siaya	1983-1988
3	Jael Oriwa Oneko (mayor)	Siaya	1988- 1992
4	Prisca Auma Misachi (mayor)	Kisumu	2002-2007
5	Onyango Radier (deputy mayor)	Kisumu	1992 - 1997

PIONEERS IN SOCIAL AND ECONOMIC SECTORS

World war 1 medalists from Uyoma were Oyieko Obuya and Okecha who served in the ranks of Regimental Sergent Major (RSM), in public transport there were Benard Oriwo Ochar from Kabudha who owned the 9 fleet Kamollo buses, Rading Akoth from Kobon who owned Mawira buses and Walter Fanuel Odede from Katwenga. Uyoma had people who could speak english very fluently these were the likes ofJjohn Mark Yongo, Jonathan Okwiri and Oriwo Ochar.

Asugo Ayungo, Nehemia Omwanda, Onyango Olot, Mirambe Afwong'o, Ongong'a Sigar, and Rading Akoth were some of uyoma people who owned shops very early, the first PHD holders from Uyoma included, Dr. Walter Odede, Dr. Odundo Ambitho and Dr. Ongo'nga Achieng.

The early trade unionist from Uyoma included Kidenda Ongalo, Jacob Ochino Ogundo And Chadwick Adongo. There were people who were well known in Uyoma for their agricultural entrepreneurship, these included Enos Arara Tinga, Odundo Aduodo, Walter Fanuel Odede and Odundo Wanyadha. Nehemiah Omwanda wa **THE MUSICIANS FROM UYOMA**

ATON MITO –
Comes from Kobong was named after famous Asian business man Mehta *Mitto who* established Asembo Bay trading Centre named Kamito. Aton is known by his popular fascinating musical songs such as.

Hera wa kod Okongo koluga

Cosma Bala Owade

Otwal Ka-Daudi and Nyamuche Ngwata whom he described as a person who could consume tanks and tanks of alcohol.

YIRO ONOKA –
Comes from Katwenga near Chianda, started his music career in late 1930s and he raised many musicians amongst them was Denis Owenda *Bul pek ka ji duogo*.

DENIS OWENDA ODALO -
Came from Katieno of Kabudha, he had a band known as Cowboys Empire Jazz Band. He was also known as Bul pek ka ji duogo (the drum is heavy from the funeral), Nanga e dhano to pesa e wuoyi. (clothing is a person and Money maketh a man) these were his translations in English.
Started his music career in 1947 after having dropped from Kaloleni Primary School. He was taught music by Yiro Konoka. Cowboy Boys Jazz Band is known for his songs like

Dud- a duda wuod Oyola

Ogolo mako ogude

Mbawi paulina

Chieng Aywagra kenda jacham piny.

AKUGA TOTO -
Comes from Kunya Kabudha, and is known to have started his music career in 1950s at a very tender age, he is remembered for his songs such;
Magi and Hellena where he sang for his wives

Adongo Kakisira .

He was once a member of Owino Misiani band.

INTERESTING STORIES FROM UYOMA

TICH NG'ATO ACHIEL TEK TA TA TA (WORKING ALONE IS DIFFICULT)

Midimbe son of Ombuoro *Midimbe Ogaga* comes from Kokwiri. He was born around 1914 and was educated at Chianda Sector School. Midimbe is populary known as *Tich ng'ato achiel tek* that team work is better than individual's work. The nick name comes from his story with Nyakongo Intermidiate School in Uyoma.

This started when the Kokwiri community got together to build a Primary School to promote education in Uyoma. Midimbe wuod Ombuoro donated land for the construction of the school and also made his contribution in various fundraising events. The school was built and even Midimbe took his children to the school. One day on his visit to the school as a parent he realized that the whole school was built of mud and grass thatched roofs. As a parent it dawned on him that the money collected for the school construction was not properly utilized and he got disturbed. He went back home a disappointed man. He had been wondering why his children had-jiggers and according to him that day he got the answer. Due to the unhygienic condition of the school the children were exposed to, jiggers, typhoid, TB, pleuleria and other airborne and waterborne diseases.

Midimbe asked himself "Is this corruption or carelessness?. *Ma en mibadhi koso jwang'ruok?* Why should we collect money and expose our children to health harzards.

A week went by during the school holiday and Midimbe went to the school, with all the madness in the world carrying fire in the bucket he started to light fire on the classrooms and one by one, he started burning the school shouting in Dholuo *Yawa Babylon wang'* Babylon is burning. The villagers were alerted by the flame and smoke that engulfed the school. As the community members put off the fire Midimbe was busy lighting more fire. In the morning, he went around the school and found that one house was not burnt and he said. "Truly truly if we were seven people we would have burnt Nyakongo to ashes." (*Dine wabed kata ji abiriyo, dine wawang'o Nyakongo pep"*) It still remains a say in Uyoma.

The members of the community took legal action against Midimbe, and when called upon by the magistrate at Siaya law courts to defend himself, Midimbe told the magistrate in Luo that "*Hawi marach ni ne atiyo kenda, dine wabed kata ji abiriyo, dine wawang'o Nyakongo pep, od lum manade mane wachoko ne pesa?* (They were lucky because l was doing it alone, had we been seven people,then the whole school would have been turned to ashes, how could we raise funds only for them to build grass thatched classrooms? Midimbe was later released on medical grounds. Later on the school management committee hired the services of a qualified mason – Mr. Absalom Ojowa, the father of Dr. Sam Ligongo and all the buildings of the school were rebuilt with ash, stones and iron sheets in other words the buildings were permanent and the hygienic conditions improved in the school.

Many people believe that Midimbe is a mad man because of this act, but I think differently, the answer could be YES and NO. It still remains a say in Uyoma that: *Tich ng'at achiel, ne omono Midimbe wang'o Nyakongo.*

From Midimbe's philosophy we learn that team wok is very vital.

MZEE OSE ONGOGO

This man came from the family of Kodiembo from Kabudha. He is the grandson of Andhoga Jabilo who was instrumental in the removal of Joasembo from Uyoma. .They were residing around Matera and Ukunja area in the present Ochieng'a Sub-location.He was widely travelled and had a lot of connections with the out side world. He went to as far as Tanzania, Suba Land and even Busoga in Uganda where he came with guards full of tsetseflies, magic and a lot of cash. He came with guards around Adola scheme and Kogonga area which was initially inhabited by the Nyakach people.He opened the guards full of tsetseflies around Kogonga and Adola and hence all the surrounding people with their livestocks were either relocated or died as a result of tsetsefly bitings.

One insteresting thing about this man with his cash notes; he one day declared a competition of boiling tea using notes *piem mar chwuako chai kod pesa* instead of firewood to prove who was richer in the area of Katieno. He stashed all the notes under the jiko *kendo* until the tea was boiled and ready for consumption .His notable children are Owenda Ose *konyi to ok nenni,* the late magician Otieno Ose and Ogallo Joash of Okunja village.

MZEE NEHEMIYA OMWANDA OSEWE

1n 1928 a young boy walked into Nairobi from Uyoma at the age of eleven years. This boy was Nehemiya Omwanda Osewe from Uyoma, Katwenga' Ranalo Village. His life in Nairobi started off as a Dobi boy ironing clothes at a relative's laundry business unit, later he under took odd jobs to survive in the new Kenyan urban town.

At the dawn of World War II he was recruited as a driver cum soldier. His first major task was to drive an army truck to Mombasa, a task that succeeded miraculously. During the War he got exposed to Burma. At the end of the War he was allocated a house at Kalololeni Estate, this estate was built for War Returnees and Senior African Civil Servants. Being a town boy, he ventured into business of selling second hand clothes, but the main products were American War left-overs. Omwanda through his War connections in Burma imported these products and opened a make shift shop at the present site of Bama Market. The products that had booming sales were Army Uniforms, Kitchen Utensils and women stockings among others. Through his connections with senior civil servants who were influncial in the Government system, he initiated the construction of Bama Market. At the completion of the building, he took four stalls for business at Bama Market and one shop at Kaloleni shopping centre. He influenced the allocation of houses to the Luo and Baluhya communities with the support of the Colonial Government. The Kikuyu community who were regarded as MAU MAUs or MAU MAU sympathizers were not allocated these houses and a few of them were left in Bahati Estate and none was allocated houses in Kaloleni, Hamza and Ofafa estates.

His close associates who were senior civil servants such as Mbotela, Hamza and Ambrose Ofafa were killed by the MAU MAU for their collaboration with the Colonial Government. Incidentally his friend Ofafa was shot when they were standing next to each other at the Bama Market.

He named the market as Bama Market because of his experience and exposure to Burma in Asia during the World War II.

Back in Uyoma a small but growing market next to his home, near *Yao Kosewe* is also named Bama Market

I remember this uncle of mine as a tall man with a walking stick which could be used as a weapon. He is also an uncle of Osewe Guda famous for his Ranalo Foods hotel in Nairobi

THE UYOMA TRICKSTARS

The Uyoma youth who got their education through the effort of the forunners like Jonathan Okwiri and with a deliberate effort of Chief Odera Akango' were the elites of those days. The reknowned trickstars were men such as Otual Ka Daudi, Adhiambo Wamola, Oyaro Oneko *Apesa wuod min Lwande* and Mbogo Okelo *Adiera maduk* the naked truth, among others. These men terrorized the Business community and Colonial Employees in a bid to embarass the Government; Among the Business Community they targeted were the Asian Community better known as Dukawallahs, they were wealthier than the African Businessmen.

The most notorious among them was Adhiambo Wamola. The famous Adhiambo Wamola once took a huge loan with a rural land guarantee of Owila Farm from a Bank where the managers were of British origin representing the Colonial Government. He presented unbeatable business plan and with eloquent English and sugar courted mouth he got the loan. He later defaulted and the Auctioneer Company owned by the Indians from Kisumu who knew the Nyanza terrain followed him up to Aram. On arrival they were given the direction to Adhiambo Wamola's home. At Ruma they found a huge sign board written "*You are now entering Owila Farm*" with 4 arrows pointing to 4 different directions reading: Kobon'g, Kabudha, Katwenga'and Kokwiri. Incidentally Owila Farm is the whole of Uyoma Location at that time inhabited by Jo-Uyoma. Adhiambo Wamola had an official bankable title deed from the Colonial Government entitled Owila farm. Incidentally Oyaro Oneko had a title deed reading Hemia Mixed Farm; Mbogo Okelo had a title reading Mandera Mixed Farm Okelodom.

Adhiambo Wamola, his friends and several people from Uyoma refused to obey the Colonial Government. They did not submit the hated Colonial Poll Tax and they were rounded up by the Chief, Jonathan Okwiri at Madiany. They were put in the Government Land Rover and were being driven to Bondo Court. When they reached Kona Ka Waka, Adhiambo politely asked the Chief if he could help himself. The driver stopped the vehicle on the road side and Adhiambo opened the door and removed his coat and requested the Chief to hold it. On his return from answering the call of nature took his coat and he put it on. Minutes later he asked the Chief in Luo, *Jatelo kendo itimri koda nadi?* Adhiambo was actually acussing the Chief of having stolen money from his pocket, he kept on insisting and with the support of the other people it became a big issue.

To resolve the issue after bitter exchange of words the Chief ordered the driver to return back to Madiany. All the *mabusu* were released and the Chief paid Adhiambo Wamola a whopping Ksh. 3,000 which was equivalent to the prize of bull at that time.

Adhiambo Wamola and his friends always played tricks on the senior Government officials and they falsefully took money from the Business Community. One time he met Fanuel Odede driving his lorry full of sisal on his way to Kisumu from Kalandin. He asked Odede for a lift and Odede told him that he could not carry him because the front seat was full and traffic do not allow passengers to be carried at the back of the lorry, Adhiambo insisted he would be comfortable at the back and so Fanuel gave him a lift. When they reached Otonglo near Kisumu the Police stopped the lorry and at inspection they found Adhiambo Wamola lying comfortably on the sisal at the back of the lorry. This time he did not get away with it, the police knew him and they gave Odede the permission to discipline him before throwing him in remand. Odede caned Adhiambo Wamola thoroughly before the police remanded him for this offense plus other criminal offenses. The next day at mid day Odede was suprised to find Adhiambo Wamola drinking with his friends at Aram market.

OGOT K'OGOT

This is the story of Ogot the son of Ogot (Known as Ogot Ka Ogot) he was born among the Kabiero family of the Katweng'a clan. He was one of the lucky boys who got primary education in Chianda School. He was even more blessed that on arrival in Nairobi he was recruited in the Second World War, his third luck is that he was recruited as a cook away from the mercy of the bullets. His recruitment followed the British experience of First World War from where the Western Kenya had produced excellent agile, athletic men who served and survived the war to return home glorioustly. Ogot Ka Got was trained as cook to serve the senior Military officers during the war, in the process he learnt and spoke excellent English and Kiswahili.

During the war Ogot Kogot and his friends were of the opinion that the war they were fighting was not in their interest. He always told his comrades that this was not a Uyoma war, leave alone African war. He used to boast that after the war he would go back to Uyoma and wedge an Uyoma war against the British. The war ended and Ogot Kogot found himself jobless in the heart of Nairobi and he forgot the Uyoma war. One thing remained clear, he hated the whitemen with a passion and he always wanted vengeance for the Africans who lost their lives in the 1st and 2nd world war, the persecution that Kenyans were going through in the hands of the British and more so the Mumbo massacre. Ogot Kogot always wanted revenge like a dog of war.

One day as he put it, the God of Owila and Omia Ramul was on his side and he got a job as a cook for an elite bachelor whiteman, a Mr.Havey.

The household was composed of Bwana (the white-man), the cat (Jaki) the puppy (Niki) and Ogot Kogot (Boi from the English word Lad or Boy). This was the order of seniority in this Kileleshwa home set-up. According to Bwana the household food supply, clothing, beddings and even bathing were carried out in this order. Ogot Kogot was fourth class citizen in this set-up and this situation ignited his loath for the whitemen.

One sunny day when Ogot Kogot got completely fed up of this dehumanizing situation he decided to end it with bhang! At around 10.00am he caught Jaki with its neck twisted it and watched it die with pleasure and amusement. He skinned it boiled it and roasted on light burning fire the way they did the roasting of beef during the war with low heat of fire. Ogot Kogot turned Jaki into a fantastic lunch befitting Bwana.

Bwana arrived home early evening feeling fatigued and hungry, he found the table well set for dinner and was delighted. Bwana ate the meal with great apetite and rested the evening with seasoned fruit salad with custard. He finally set the dinner befitting Kingly ritual with black coffee and sipped while listening to the seven o'clock news. Ogot Kogot came to the table unusually polite and disappeared to the Servant Quarters.

Suddenly Bwana shouted on top of his voice as if Boi was deaf.

Bwana: *Boi wapi wewe (Boy Where are you?)*

Boi: *Bwana niko hapa (Boss I am here)*

Bwana: *Wapi Jaki (Where is Jaki?)*

Boi: *Bwana Kwani hiyo Ume Kula ni Mama yako au Jaki (Boss, the meal you have eaten is either your mother or Jaki??)*

Bwana: *Boi kuja hapa kumbafu (Boy don't be stupid)*

Boi: *Wewe ndiyo kumbafu. Ume kula paka yako (You are the one who is stupid; you have eaten your cat)*

The house went on fire when Bwana jumped on the Boi's neck and hit him twice on the face, Boi shouted 'Bwana don't kill me". The neigbours heard the Boi's painfull cry and people ran to his help. As people came to the boi's help he turned round like a dog of war and he beat Bwana mercilessly and senselessly befitting hospital bed. Ogot Kogot left the job unceremoniously, with great satisfaction after having thrushed the white bastard as bosted later.

Ogot Kogot was charged for assault but was acquitted for having been on self defence and as such there was no case to answer and all the Africans refused to give witness. The lack of witnesses was the evidence of the hate and loathe of Africans for the Whiteman and their British rule.

Ogot Kogot used to say that he would make hell for the British in vengeance for the Mumbo Massacre in Uyoma.

Ogot Kogot would visit the hotels in Nairobi that were no-go for Africans and pick up any small quarrel and make a commotion and ensure a fight erupted to give a chance to create a fight and since he was well trained for fighting during the war, he would senslessly beat up his opponents. The hotels' management would try to make a cover-up to avoid adverse publicity.

Ogot Kogot was an advocate for Kenya or African Freedom and investment where-ever they could, instead of being treated as third class citizen or strangers in their own backyard.

He kept on wondering why Africans would cook good meals and yet they were not allowed to eat that food or even serve other fellow Africans.

Ogot Kogot hated what he called Whiteman's Christianity and he denounced his Anglican Religion and joined Islam which he viewed to be more African.

Mr. Einsworth caught up with Ogot Kogot and convinced him to take a job in the Europeans farms, this apeassed him for sometime. Ogot Kogot could not settle and he moved to Kisumu town where he joined KANU youth activits under the leadership of Oruko Makasembo.

Ogot Kogot also served as a house help for Jaramogi Oginga Odinga in Kisumu where Raila and Oburu constantly complained of his ruthlessness.

He died peacefully in 1969 but controvesy followed him to his death, this time it was whether his body should be buried in Muslim cementry in Kisumu or in his ancestral land in Uyoma behind the Mumbo Massacre scene. Jo-Uyoma prevailed and he was buried in Uyoma.

The living offsprings of Ogot Kogot are William Sembe Ogot, Elisha Aete Ogot and Odongo Ogot who are still living at Mumbo in Lieta in South Uyoma.

That is Ogot Kogot!

THE RISE OF JARAMOGI OGINGA ODINGA FROM UYOMA

One day a young boy in standard four was assigned the task of slaughtering four hens to make a meal without realizing that he was a party to the making of Kenyan history in regard to the doyen of the opposition Jaramogi Oginga Odinga.

The story started in Aram when Vitalis Asugo called upon his nephew Alex Odie to make a meal for their visitors. The visitors that arrived were Apollo Ohanga (A nominated member of Legico, from Gem) Arina Oulo (A DC in Kisii from Uyoma), Oginga Odinga (A Businessman in Kisumu from Sakwa), Odindo Nyasaka (an employee with the Ministry of Agriculture from Uyoma) and the host Mr. Asugo a businessman in Aram also from Uyoma. After the meal the discussion that took place was as follows, Mr. Asugo was given the duty to Chair the meeting. The agenda of the meeting entailed the 1957 election that was to take place to replace the Colonial Government nomination which saw Apollo Ohanga as the Nyanza representative. All the personalities in the room were potential candidates for Legico and also age mates or contemporaries and gone through Maseno School as students or teachers. The issue was to agree on a single candiadate among the four personalities. The summary of the discussion was that:

Mr. Arina was a seasoned administrator who could and had made much contribution in the development of the Luo community therefore the rationale to join politics was unnecessary far fetched issue.

Mr. Odindo was a technocrat who was a useful personality in regard to agricultural intervention which the Luo needed now and even after independence.

Hon. Ohanga had a nomination and was very friendly to the Colonial Government and the Luo community needed that strategic linkage with the existing Government even after independence.
Mr. Odinga was Ker (Ceremonial leader) of Luo which was a social position and leaning towards politics. He was incharge of Luo commercial ventures while Oneko was the one spear heading the Luo political wing. Mr. Odinga's mother comes from Uyoma Kagwa. Even his name originates from Chief Oginga Agidhi.

The Chairman made his contribution by proposing the following:

You are all very good candidates but if we do not have one candidate the Luo community will lose the Nyanza Legislative Council slot, therefore I propose the following:

Mr. Arina and Mr. Odindo should continue making their contribution to the development of the Luo community and leave this political office to Mr. Ohanga and Mr. Odinga. One Mr. Ohanga is a blue eyed boy of the Colonial Government and if he doesn't contest the elections he will definitely be appointed or be nominated to Legco based on his past performance record. He joked and said my friend Mr. Odinga is currently jobless and should be given the opportunity to contest for the following reasons. Most Kenyans will support him because of his association with Jomo Kenyatta and Achieng' Oneko, Jo-Uyoma I'm sure will support him because of Mr. Okwiri and the two leading personalities in this room. Lastly Uyoma will support him because Uyoma would have supported Odede due to his national position as the last Chairman of KAU replacing Jomo Kenyatta, but Mr. Odinga has said that he will step aside for Odede upon Odede's release from detention, a promise which he never honoured.

At this point Mr. Ohanga protested and vowed to go it alone; he actually remarked that he was surprised that the meeting had turned into an Uyoma affair. Mr. Asugo concluded that in his mind he was fair but everybody is entitled to their opinion. Mr. Ohanga left the meeting earlier and promised Mr. Odinga a battle of the giants. After Ohanga's exit Asugo requested Mr. Odinga to go and pass the resolutions of this meeting and while consulting Jo-Sakwa (home ground), Jo-Alego (your in-laws), Kisumu (your work place) and then move flat out into South Nyanza, Kisii and among the Luhya. You don't need to come to Uyoma we will set the ball rolling with speed as from tomorrow.

Jaramogi Oginga Odinga's political journey started in Aram in 1957 and he climbed the political ladder and ended to the pinnacle in 1994 when he passed on as the longest living leader of the opposition nick named the Doyen of opposition politics in Kenya.

At the end of the story, I asked Jaduong Odie how he could remember this story, he told me that, "My son I was in School and Uyoma apart from the rest of the country was politicaly charged. There was fear of MAU MAU especially the detention of Walter Fanuel Odede and Ramogi Achirng' Oneko which was common knowledge and discussed everywhere and anywhere in Uyoma.'

Jo-uyoma loved and cherished them.

SHRINES AND HISTORICAL SITES IN UYOMA

GOT NAYA

The eastern side view of Got Naya

The land mark of Uyoma is visible even from Rang'ala in Ugenya, Got Ng'iya in Alego, Got Ramogi in Yimbo, Homa Bay in Homay Bay County and other places; this was the site of rituals for Jo-Uyoma. During the return from Kawango this was the point that Owila used to give his kinsmen direction as the site of the ancestral land. It is found in South Uyoma near Luanda Kotieno Beach which is the gate way to Mbita Island. This is where the Uyoma Water Project is situated because it is also the highest point in Uyoma.

RIMU MATARA

This was where the Uyoma people led by Andhoga the magician *jabilo* did the sacrifice that removed the Kale *Asembo* a way from Uyoma .

The site is found just behind Koyaro Oneko home in Kunya Village, Rageng'ni Sub- Location.The egyptica tree *otho* is found as the land mark.

NYAMARIMBA

This is a very interesting site. There were a male and female *egyptica/otho* trees with all the signs of human biological sexual organs Jo-Uyoma used to give offerings at the site during times of pestilences and catastrophies. The Uyoma elders held a meeting with the representative of the British colonial government Mr. Odera Ulalo on the need for Jo-Uyoma to provide food and other materials towards the construction of the Kenya Uganda Railway which had reached Lumbwa. This meeting is the origin of the Mumbo massacre.The site is found on the Western side of Rageng'ni Centre at Kabaka Aloo's home.

MUMBO

Mumbo is an area found in Lieta sub-location, South Uyoma it is inhabited by Katweng'a and Kabuong' clans. It is a very important area because it was where the Canoe which carried the magical concoction from Kanyamwa landed on the return to Uyoma from Kanyamwa .One of Owila's grandchildren Oluoch Abaki lived here. It was where the Uyoma people assembled on 27th December 1899 during the forceful entry of the white man into Uyoma. People were killed livestocks were consficated by force .It is the site of Mumbo massacre.

RAGENG'NI

This is now one of the biggest market centres in Uyoma with thriving business. There are several bars, hotels, shops, Churches, Administration Centre and other horticultural products. The centre is accesible from all directions of corners through tarmac and weather roads.All the roads to the beaches of East and South Uyoma connect. The center has both electricity and clean piped water, hospital facility and pharmacetical shops. It is the bussiest trading centre in Rarieda sub County.The place is called Rageng'ni because the Uyoma people were hindered or obstructed from accessing the Eastern water point by the *Gem Kanyitondo* people when the Jo Uyoma returned from Kawango.

OWIMBI.

Owimbi centre is found between Gagra and Ruma the Kale and Kakia people used to reside in this place before. It used to be called Pedo Village.During the reign of Chief Otumba Mbede and Adhola of Uyoma and Asembo respectively. There were thugs or suspects *Achije* who were brought to this place by the British Government on transit to the Island in South Nyanza .The DC by then was Mr. Wainright.The place was named to have belonged to the people who were on transit *Joma Owimbi* .

This place served as the Uyoma location headquarter *chief camp* until 1955 when chief Bathlomeow s Nyabola Owiti moved it to Manyuanda just as *The Great Britain Government also moved suspects or thugs to Austrailia.*

RUMA

Ruma is between Aram and Owimbi and is found in Masala sublocation. It was earlier inhabited by Jo – Kisumu. The Uyoma warriors who had participated in chasing the Kales past Rarieda school while returning met Jo-Uyoma who were curious to know the results of the war. The warriors replied that the war/ exercise is over *orumo* hence the name **RUMA**.

EVERY NAME HAS A MEANING

Every name has a meaning and it's origin.
Luos name places, people and even institutions according the Geographical factors, historical events both social and political, technological inventions and people among others.
Let us look at some names and origins of some of the places and sites in Uyoma

ARAM.

During the chief trainship of Oginga Agidhi, of Uyoma, there were skirmishes between the Jo-Uyoma and Asembo. The Asembo were chased away from Uyoma but when the chase reached river Miho, they vowed not to move any further. *Aram*o is a Luo word meaning vow and hence the name Aram.

CHIANDA.

Chianda is the cradle for civilization and the relevance to Jo Uyoma. When Jo Uyoma settled their from Mumias they came from the place called Shihanda and hence Chianda according to the British pronunciation.

GAGRA.

Gagra is a small shopping centre along the Kisumu-Luanda Kotieno road. It is the equicentre of Rarieda sub-county. The place is predominantly inhabited by the Kotwal sub-clan of Kobong'. The centre hosts both primary and secondary schools and a catholic church which is a stone throw on the junction to Madiany.

When Jo-Uyoma were on their sojourn back from Kawango after a short stay in Alego Kobare, they arrived at this place at around noon and had a luncheon– *migago* before they crossed river Mawira to Thurmony, Madiany. The name Gagra is derived from the word *gago* and the British corrupted the pronounciation to Gagra

KUNYA.

Kunya can also be refered to as Sori, these two words mean peninsula in English.

KOGONGA.

Ogonga was a famous fisherman from Nyakach who settled around Nyamasore. Ogonga had his own beach when Ose Ongogo came with tsetsefly he moved to west Uyoma in the present bar Kogonga primary school.

LUANDA KOTIENO.

Otieno the son of Ousa, who was a very famous Sigulu man who settled at the Southern most part of Uyoma. He had a disease of hitches on his body and when fishermen went down the lake, he was always seen warming himself on the rock and hence Luanda Kotieno which means the rock of Otieno.

MANYUANDA.

This is a place where people of different clans leave.at Manyuanda there are the; Kagwa, Kagoro, Katwenga and Kokwiri Kabuong'.

MISORI.

Misori is a Luo word which means physical projection of a piece of land into the sea. The place Misori in West Uyoma is a beach which is projected inside the lake.

NAYA

The place was originaly inhabited by the Banyalla and they named the hill as IInaya, but Luos call it Naya Kogweno for historical reasons. The Kogweno people of Karachuonyo inhabited the area for a short period of time. Got Naya is the highest point in Uyoma.

OSINDO.

The word is derived from *sindo* which means refusal.The cattle of Omia Ramul were being refused to drink water at lake shore in western Uyoma by kobunga people and hence Osindo.

OWIMBI.

The original and historical name is Pedo. But rebels and stock thieves posed a security risk in Asembo and were being deported to the desolate South Nyanza by order of chief native commissioner, Mr Weinright with the blessings of chief Adhola of Asembo. When they reached Uyoma, chief Otumba settled them. The Luo word 'wimbo' means temporary settlement. The Asembo people who settled in that part of Uyoma named that place Owimbi to date

RACHAR.

Rachar is the original name of the place. During drought season, you could only see the place as white, hence the name Rachar. It was formerly inhabited by the Sakwa untill the Uyoma chased Sakwa away.

RAGENG'NI.

After the incident at Osindo in West Uyoma, Omia Ramul then turned Eastwards at a place near Nyamarimba which was inhabited by the Gem Kanyidoto people. Omia Ramul was prevented or hindered from passing with his cattle through to the lake shore to drink water. The act of preventing Omia Ramul's cattle moving eastwards is known in Luo as *Geng'o'* hence the word Rageng'ni.

MADIANY.

The problems Omia Ramul faced in Uyoma at Osindo in west Uyoma and Rageng'ni to the east made the place which was initially known as Thurmony to be named Madiany, the place of bewilderment.

The general problem was that Omia Ramul was at the center or the middle of Uyoma. Although Uyoma is almost surrounded by the mass of water, the hinterland is dry almost nine months annually. Omia Ramul was stuck and could not move because of hostility of the inhabitants, drought and famine. He had nowhere to turn/move to east or west, North or south were all blocked for their cattle to access water points hence Madiany- the situation bewildered him. Today it's the administrative center of Uyoma.

WAYAGA.

Before Uyoma people migrated to South Nyanza, the present Islet of Wayaga was part of the main land. It was more or less an Isthmass. Koyoo people of Katweng'a settled there but when Uyoma people returned, Opao and Ongili were targeting to reach and settle at their ancestral home at Wayaga. They could not locate it because the isthmus had physically become an islet, so where they settled they called it Wayaga to date in east Katweng'a.

KOBONG'.

Obong' was a remnant of Kanyada people who were living in the present Pala Kobong' primary school. He remained behind when the Kanyada people were moving to the present Homabay county.

When the Uyoma people migrated from Kawango, the families of Omolo, Okelo and Otwal went to Obong's home while the Kabudha, Katweng'a, Kajore and Kokwiri went to live near Nyabera.

The Komolo, Kokelo and Kotwal went and stayed at Obong's home. They were being referred to Jo-kobong', the Obong's. The name remains to date.

RANYALA

Ranyala is found in Naya sublocation-South Uyoma. The Manyala people inhabited this place along the lakeshore of Lake Victoria on the foot of Got Naya which was called Iinaya but corruptly called Naya by the Luos. Ranyala primary school is named in honour of the patriarchs of the Manyala clan who were living there.

JO-KABUDHA

Odero was one of Ojal's wives and she is the grandmother of Jo-Kabudha. The word Abudha is Odero's nick name. It originates from the way she performed her domestic chores, she was careless. In general her house and even kitchen was not well kept. *Odero ne dhako ma nyuandre makata ka idonjo e ode to ok inyal ng'eyo pogruok mar dier ot, korka mach kata agola. Koro Jo-Kabudha ipako ni obuth manyonge*

NO LEADERSHIP FOR NUSU KARNE (HALF A CENTURY)

In 1977, Martin Okayo Achola of Got Kachola told me "*Kijana yangu, Nusu Karne ita pita na hamta pata uongozi*"

In my early youth my father sent me to collect a carpet for Ragengni Church, (St. Johns). I drove the red Toyota pick up exited because I knew I was going to drive all the way to Uyoma carrying this carpet. Jaduong Achola was working in Juja and I arrived in his office at 11.00am as per the appointment.

He greeted me with all the joy a nephew deserves. He had organized for an open air lunch facing Thika Road. We sat for the meal and exchanged lots of ideas and stories. One story will never escape my mind.

Achola: "*My son, do you see that branching road from Thika road?*"

Lwande: *Yes I can see it and incidentally I know it, it goes to the Presidents home*

Achola: *Good, you are well informed*

Lwande: *No, this is a home I have visited severally*

Achola: *My son I am praying 'Kijana yangu, Nusu Karne ita pita na hamuta pata uongozi" A Luo*

  Shall not become President for the next fifty years and beyond.

Lwande: *Why uncle?*

Achola: *All the people going to Gatundu and those living there are drunk with alcohol but more with power. If Luos gets this Presidency, they will be drunk and the community will not be able to contain the drunkardness. Your people are drunk with out power when they get power they will be super dead drunk. Wata lewa kupindukia*

Kenya's first President Mzee Jomo Kenyatta made similar remarks in Kisumu in 1966 after Luo mass exodus from Jomo Kenyatta regime to form KPU (Kenya Peoples Union). "*Nyinyi Wajaluo mukiendelea tu, na mademonstration yenu, Kisii and Wakalenjin wata washinda kwa umbali, saa hizi muna ringa ya kwamba mume soma. Chungeni Wakenya wote watasoma na watakuwa na maendeleo kuwashinda.*"

This book is written 50 years after these sentiments. Luos have not ascended to leadership, true or false?

One day it will come to pass and one of our offsprings will take over Kenyan leadership.

Ok nyal bet ni wan wasembo jomoko to wan to wadong' chien.

Hatuwezi kuwa kama makanga ya matatu anae sema twende kisha ana baki nyuma

Even today as I write this book the Luo community is very far from State House in this Karne

First the Luos celebrate Victory before Victory. Gin gi ng'eyo ni *Gini wase kawo*

The Luos are great Warriors and Gladiators in the Battlefield

They are not great leaders and Strategists at leadership level

They think politics is a football match where there is no take home.

The chronological history tells us that Luo Community was in the political forefront right from 1900.

During the 1920s and beyond Jonathan Okwiri Nyakinya led Luo agitation for independence.

During the struggle for Independence in the 1950s, Walter Fanuel Odede had a chance for top National seat but him and Jaramogi Oginga odinga started power struggle for village supremacy and they both lost the large picture.

At the dawn of Independence the Luo community had the most powerful positions in the Nation. Then Tom Mboya and Oginga odinga started a Luo house hold power struggle giving room for other communities to take advantage. They both lost and Ramogi Achieng Oneko lost his opportunity of Vice Presidency.

During the 1982 coup Luo leaders were in the battle field as foot soldiers and many of them remained in the war trenches.

The political scenario of 1990s remains a shamble with no strategies; it was just a people wallowing through political turbulences.

In 2000 and beyond Raila Amolo Odinga the lone ranger used party vehicles to ascend to State house but in vain

And so:

Jonathan Okwiri Nyakinya later succumbed to death a forgotten hero with his chin on his palms

Fanuel Odede Obonyo towered to national leadership but died skimping towards Parliament

Thomas Joseph Mboya died at the mercy of an assassin's gun while playing tactics towards KANU supremacy

Jaramogi Oginga Odinga died a wounded duck yawning for a helping hand to State House, he was nick named the doyen of opposition in Kenya

Ramogi Achieng Oneko died hands down on his lap at the bosom of Nyanza Gulf in his rural home, he was nick named a national Hero

Raila Amolo Odinga fought many battles but did not reach the finishing touch. He kept falling behind the enemy line into the realms of opposition

These are the Luo stallions of the twentieth century

We have been in the opposition from 1900 to 2015

We have only been in Government for three years 1963 to 1966

In Luo land if you work with the sitting Government you are labeled a traitor.

Yet the Government is every Nation's Cash Cow.

Do we now have to wait for another whole Karne?

Maru ni ok bulie ng'or chiegi?

Thuondwagi oa mana nono komako tikgi

Licking their wounds

THE UYOMA ANTHEM

Uyoma there anthem compossed by Henry Onditi Achola ,this anthem used to be sang whenever the Uyoma elders were going to pray and offer scarifies at places such as Got Naya. The anthem was as follows ;

2. *Otimbla ochako piny ne Jo-Uyoma*
   Uyoma pogore tienge abich
3. *Katwenga en dhoot kama otingo Odede Obonyo*
   Odede en japuonj manopuonjo Makere
4. *Kabudha en dhoot kama Otingo Achieng' Oneko*
   Achieng en jabura manochako KAU
5. *Kobong en dhoot kama otingo Arina Oulo*
   Arina Oulo en DC matiyo Kericho.
6. *Kokwiri en dhoot kama otingo Ongiri Ongili*
   Ongiri en jathieth matiyo Maseno Hospital.
7. *Kagwa en dhoot kama otingo Owiti Opany.*
   Owiti en japuonj mapuonjo e school Nyakongo.
8. *Ruodh Rawila machon en Otumba Mbede*
   Otumba ne en Ruoth majabilo .
   Otumba otiyo Ruoth bange oweyo ne moyi.
   Moyi en Ruoth mane opayo ndara
   Moyi otiyo oweyo no Ojungo,
   Ojungo e Ruoth mane Ochungo Chianda
   Ojungo Otiyo Ruoth bange oweyo ne Okwiri,
   Okwiri en ruoth ma piny noyiego teee!!!.Amen.

FACILITATORS

Debora Akinyi Haggai, Harun Ouro Oyuga, Charles Otieno Ogonda, Peter Awich Oyaro, Elizabeth Omondi, Henry Opiyo and Bernard Owigo

Some of the Uyoma Elders consulting at the home of Ramogi Achieng' Oneko during tea break at the validation workshop in April 2014;L;-R-Haggai Angira,Were,Mariko Odipo ,Agripa Ojuka and Anyumba Nyamor

Validation workshop participants in Kunya April 2014

Validation workshop participants are led by Lwande Oneko from Ramogi Achieng's mauseleum

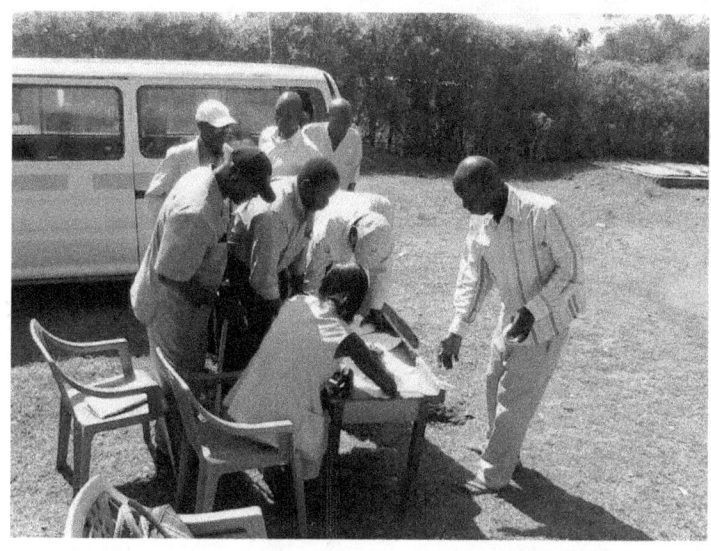

Participants in the validation workshop being helped at the registration desk by Peter Oyaro and Debora Akinyi (Seated)

Mzee Zakayo Abonyo Oyombe during the validation workshop. Zakayo comes from kagwa and was a renowned Great Magician and a Political Leader. This was his last public appearance, he died in May 2014.

Harun Ouro Oyuga facilitating the validation workshop at Kunya Uyoma.

Mzee Apollo Washington Juma Otito – key informant in the documentation room

SUCCESS CORNERSTONES

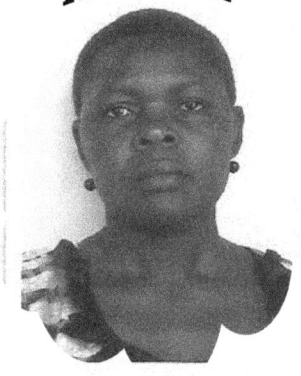

Ruth Owuor

Documented the draft manuscript

Jack Owenda

Keenly drafted the primary data and collected secondary information

Kola Midundo

Linked us to a network of more than 100 beacons who were the key informants for primary data

REFERENCE BOOKS.

1. Dhoudi Moko Mag Luo by Shadrack Malo.
2. Thuond Luo by Mayor, A.M.
3. A History of Egypt and the Nile Valley from Ancient Times by Prof. W.R Ochieng'.
4. A History by Western Kenya in The 20th and 21st centuaries
5. A History of the Luo Speaking People of Eastern Africa By Ogot B.A
6. The Luo –The Black Jewis of Africa-By Alanyo George William
7. My Journey With Jaramogi - by Odinge Odera
8. The Kapenguria Six-By Wanyiri Kihoro
9. Luo Origin and politics;Emergence of nilotic Luo in 1000 AD and after-BY George W Otieno Adede
10. A History of Indipendent Kenya-Ed BY prof Ochieng'
11. Report on the Uyoma expedition near lake Victoria by C.W Hobley
12. Kenya; From chartered company to Crown Colony 2nd Edition by C.W Hobley
13. A History of the Luo of South Nyanza-BY Ayot, T.O
14. A History of the Jo-Karachuonyo by Olang' David Owiti Dulo
15. The Luo Tribes and Clans by Evans Pritchard E.E
16. The Luo By Sandandrea S.
17. A Tribal History of the Bahr-el-Ghazal
18. The articulation of the Luo ethnic citizenship; the Case of Achieng' Oneko Ramogi.- by Ogude J.kenya,
19. The articulation of Luo Ethnic citizenship; the case of Achieng'Oneko Ramogi; current writings 13(2):43-56, 2001.
20. A history of the Luo-Abasuba of Western Kenya literature Bureau, Nairobi Kenya 1979.
21. A history of the southern Luo vol.1 –B.A Ogot 1967.
22. A history of the Luo-speaking people's of Easten Africa –B.A Ogot.
23. A history of the Kenya peoples' union 1966-1969 - Paul Okello Ogula, MA thesis. Makerere University 1977.
24. The flame of freedom – Sarah Elderkim
25. Decolonization and independence in Kenya – B.A Ogot and Ochieng' WR 1940 -1993 – Nairobi.
26. Ogutu, G.E.M. Ker in the 21st century Luo social system, Sundowner Press, Kisumu, 2009.
27. The Kenya African Union, London and Boston 1985.
28. Colonial Families in Luo land; Kenya 1905-1945; staff seminar paper, KUSP series, 25th February.
29. Not yet Uhuru – Oginga Odinga, 1967.
30. British Administration in Central Nyanza District of Kenya, 1900-1960. In journal of African History Vol.4 – B.A Ogot.
31. Kenya Government Statement on the arrest of Walter Odede, detained KAU leader, Press office Handouts, March 9, 1953 East African Standard.
32. Ref. Ogot B.A The Jii – speaking peoples of Eastern Africa
33. Ref. Malo Shadrack. Dhoudi Mag Central Nyanza

34. Ref. Hobley, C.W "Nilotic Tribes of Kavirondo" in Eastern Uganda

35. The flame of freedom by Raila Odinga

www.ingramcontent.com/pod-product-compliance
Lightning Source LLC
Chambersburg PA
CBHW081014040426

42444CB00014B/3198